# Birds
## IN THE
# Belfry

*Raelene Phillips*
*Matthew 6:26*

Other books in the *All God's Creatures* series:

*Cats in the Parsonage* by Clair Shaffer, Jr.

*Cats in the Parsonage II* by Clair Shaffer, Jr.

*Puppy in the Pulpit* by Raelene Phillips

# Birds
## IN THE
# Belfry

## Raelene Phillips

**E**vergreen
PRESS

ISBN  1-58169-187-4
For Worldwide Distribution
Printed in the U.S.A.

Evergreen Press
P.O. Box 191540 • Mobile, AL 36619
800-367-8203

*Editor's Note: Names have been changed to protect the privacy of the individuals mentioned.*

# TABLE OF CONTENTS

# DEDICATION

This book is lovingly dedicated to the memory of
the first bird I ever really cared about:
Bimbo Wood

I would also like to dedicate the book
to the memory of:

Rev. Richard Black
1941-2005

Pastor Dick taught me so much about
birds during our brief stay in their home.
Without his help, I doubt this book would
have ever been written.
We will miss you, but we know that
earth's loss is heaven's gain.

# INTRODUCTION

I wish I had learned the fun hobby of bird watching when I was much younger. But perhaps God has allowed me to discover His darling little creatures at this stage in my life for some distinct reasons. Perhaps He knows that there are times when I just need to slow down and enjoy listening to them sing—ever reminded of the promise found in Song of Solomon 2:12 that after a time of sadness "the time of the singing of birds is come." Perhaps He knows that there are times when I am feeling of little value and need to remember the words of His Son who taught in Matthew 10:29-31 that not one bird falls to the ground apart from His will. He ends that admonition with "Do not fear therefore: you are of more value than many sparrows." A closer reading of that scripture shows us that perhaps the first birdwatcher is God Himself!

Though birds are some of the smallest of the creatures God created, it seems that He thinks they are pretty important. They are mentioned many times in scripture, and almost always in a positive light. So, now that my Mom has taught me the joy of watching these little creatures, I began to wonder if there were principles of life that we could learn from observing birds. So I began to jot down some thoughts, and this book is the final result.

As I watch how the birds relate to each other and view the interplay between them, I have often been reminded of the old proverb: Birds of a feather flock together. I have found this to be amazingly accurate. Each different species seems to find its own kind, though at times there are as many as six different types of bird at my small feeder. It never ceases to amaze me how they care for "their own" and fight to protect their kind from the others.

As I relate this proverb to the grander scale of human interplay, I have often joked that while birds of a feather flock together it would appear that all too often "birds of the Father (people) don't want to bother." Okay, I never claimed to be a poet. My husband chuckles that I should not give up my day job to go into poetry. But, if we think of ourselves as the "birds of the Father," I really feel there is much we can learn from quiet observation of our feathered friends.

And so, I hope you will put your chair near an open window—preferably one with a bird feeder nearby—and sit back and enjoy my musings about the *Birds in the Belfry.* But if you should hear a different song than you've heard before, lay the book down and quietly grab a pair of binoculars. For the birds can teach you much more than I ever will!

Happy reading!
*Raelene Phillips*

Chapter One

# Canaries & Goldfinches

S ome of my earliest memories involve a bird. In one corner of our dining room, when I was growing up, hung a cage that housed Dicky, my mother's canary. Dicky's main accomplishment in life was tenaciously doing what he was born to do, every day—singing his little heart out. It was a pleasing mixture of many high notes on the musical scale. His song was music to my mother's ears, and she never tired of hearing him. What was happening in the rest of the world never mattered to Dicky. He just sang along merrily, ignoring the cold war that seemed to threaten the end of life as we knew it in 1950s America.

Since Dicky never was let out of his cage, I didn't have

1

much interaction with him. I do remember, however, that Mom taught me at an early age how to pick out the certain type of wide-leafed dandelion greens that the bird loved to eat. These greens grew wild in the little patch of lawn between the sidewalk and our house, just under our kitchen window. Mom would say, "Raelene, let's give Dicky a treat today." I would run outside and pick one or two of the plant's leaves, bring them inside, and gingerly hold them up to Dicky's cage. He would sing enthusiastically as he took them from my little five-year-old fingers and spend the next several hours devouring the leaves with glee. It was fun to be able to feed the little songster.

Molting was a problem that periodically caused my mom to worry about Dicky. He would stop singing, puff out all his feathers, and sit resolutely on his perch. Eventually he lost some of his feathers. During these times, Mom always put a lightbulb in his cage and covered the cage with cloth on the outside (for warmth, I suppose). She brought Dicky through this periodic phenomenon with help from the pet store or a veterinarian on more than one occasion. Evidently molting was the way the canary grew new feathers. His song stopped for a brief period of time as he fought to get rid of the old feathers and grow new ones. Without this process, the bird would have died, but as soon as the old feathers had fallen out and new ones had been added, he sang again at the top of his little lungs.

When it came time for our family's annual camping vacation, it took quite a bit of planning. Dicky the canary and Bimbo our parakeet were loaded into the car and hauled to the home of my cousin Dortha, who "bird-sat" for us. Tammy, our cat, was more self-reliant, and all she needed was someone to feed her, give her water, and clean her litter box. So, once all of this was cared for, we were off to Gun Lake, Michigan, and Yankee Springs State Park campground.

# The Goldfinches

We spent two glorious weeks lounging around a campsite, complete with tent, tarpaulin to shade our picnic table and cooking area, and a fire ring for nightly campfires. Those days were so very different from our normal lives in the city. We enjoyed swimming, boating, waterskiing, hiking, and total relaxation in God's amazing world of nature.

One of the reasons Mom absolutely loved Gun Lake was because the entire area was overrun with what she called "wild canaries." Those little yellow birds seemed to be everywhere, and we often woke up to the sound of their song and fell asleep for afternoon naps listening to the same notes. They sounded so much like Dicky that it felt like an invisible link back to our home on Atlantic Avenue. For no matter how wonderful our vacation time was, Mom was always a homebody, glad to get back to the routines of "normal life."

Years later, after the demise of Dicky, and when our camping days were only a memory, Mom became an avid bird-watcher. It was only then that she found out her "wild canaries" were really American goldfinches. The male bird is bright yellow in the summertime and sports a black cap, tail, and wings. He is a strikingly beautiful little bird. His female counterpart is not as brightly-colored as he, but both sing the beautiful Dicky-like song. These birds do not migrate south, no matter how horrible our Ohio winter, so they are some of the rare birds that we can watch year-round. In the winter, Mr. Goldfinch's bright yellow coat turns paler, which makes him look like his wife.

Other than their song, perhaps the most easily distinguishable characteristic of the American goldfinch is their flight pattern. They never fly directly to the wire or tree that is their final destination (perhaps they never studied geometry to learn that the shortest distance between two points is a straight line). No, their flight makes one think of a roller-coaster. For their bodies seem to bounce up and down, going over imaginary hills as they fly. As I watch them fly, I wonder what might be the reason for their strange, bouncing flight. The one thing that is apparent is that they love doing it, for they nearly always sing or call out "per-chick-o-ree" as they fly.

In order to attract these little birds to our yard, I purchased a finch feeder. This is a tube of clear plastic filled with thistle seed. There are four dowel rods that go through the tube, protruding just far enough on each side for the little birds to perch on. A tiny hole, the size of one thistle seed, is strategically placed at just the right distance from the perch, so that our bouncy, little yellow friends can reach the food. I wanted to have goldfinches coming to my feeder to remind me of my long ago-friend Dicky and the "wild canaries" of our yearly jaunts to Gun Lake.

Much to my dismay, other birds began to push out the goldfinches. There were birds of all varieties around, and yes, I wanted to feed every one of them, but my favorites were the goldfinches. They seemed to be too shy to "duke it out" with the larger birds for their food. In my despair, I called Mom. "The other birds are nudging out the goldfinches. What can I do?" I wailed.

With a familiar chuckle in her voice, she instructed me to get another tube-like feeder. "It is built exactly the same," she said, "but it will have the words upside down on the box." Another trip to the store yielded the infamous "Upside Down Goldfinch Feeder." We filled it with thistle seed and hung it near the first feeder.

Within just a few hours, every station on the new tube had a goldfinch happily feeding away. And they were hanging upside down from the perches to do so! We were spellbound. My husband and I watched and wondered how it was possible to swallow food while hanging upside down. Another call to Mom, the resident bird expert, ensued.

"How do they do it?" I asked. "And, more importantly, why do the other birds leave them alone at this feeder?"

Mom laughed again as she replied, "I don't have any idea why it works. Evidently God made the beautiful little goldfinches capable of eating upside down. And the other birds are heavier than the goldfinches, so they cannot hang upside down, even long enough to get one seed. I never have worried about why it works. I am just thankful that it does."

Once again, my mother's wisdom came through loud and clear. She didn't have to know why; she just knew what worked and accepted it.

## Singing With Abandon

Learning to live with Dicky as a child, and then watching the American goldfinches as an adult, has taught me several important lessons. Both species of birds sing for all they are worth. It makes no difference what else is going on in their little bird worlds. They were given the task of providing music for their segment of creation, and they do so with abandon. Perhaps they stop for awhile during a molting season, as Dicky did, but once their body is feeling all right again, they warble away.

As a teenager I learned a chorus which included the words, "Sing when the day is bright, sing in the darkest night, every day, all the way, let us sing, sing, sing!" In the Psalms we are often encouraged to sing. And in the book of Job, the author refers to God as the giver of "songs in the night" (Job 35:10, NIV).

## A Land Far Away

In Psalm 137, there is a story that makes me think of the differences between canaries or goldfinches and me. The children of Israel had been carried away captive into Babylon. The writer of the psalm relates that in Babylon, the captives sat down and wept and hung their harps upon the willows. It appears that they did not plan to sing anymore. They were bitter and sad. The Babylonians asked the Israelites to sing a song for them, saying, "Sing us one of the songs of Zion!" (vs. 3). They wanted the children of Israel to entertain them with one of their folk songs or perhaps a hymn to their God. However, the Israelites refused and said, "How shall we sing the Lord's song in a foreign land?"

When Dan and I were first married, he was in the U.S. Navy. He was stationed at Whidbey Island, Washington. We loaded all our worldly possessions into our Volkswagen Bug and drove from Ohio to Washington. We were awestruck by the beauty of the mountains and the Pacific Northwest. Seattle sits on the Puget Sound like a jewel against the backdrop of Mt. Rainier. Whidbey is an amazing little island out in the Sound, filled with quaint little fishing villages and wonderful rocky shorelines. We should have been as happy as the proverbial larks to be allowed to live in such a wonderful place.

However, I was very pregnant, very scared, and very homesick for my parents and the family we had left behind in Ohio. Instead of enjoying the wonderful insect-free environment and beautiful mountain vistas, I pouted that God had allowed me to be "carried captive" so far away from my home.

We began to attend a little Nazarene church in Oak Harbor, Washington. The fellowship was sweet. When I could get my mind off my homesickness, I began to enjoy life again. The music in this church was more upbeat than I was used to. The organist used the drum attachment to the organ and the people almost danced as they sang, but not quite. I guess a more accurate description would be that we swayed a little to the beat. One favorite song in that hymnal was "This Is Like Heaven to Me." The lyrics were about how fellowship with like-minded believers was like a little taste of heaven. While I enjoyed the tune, in my stubborn way I would refuse to sing this song.

Dan asked me why I would not join in when the church sang that song. I informed him that being in Washington State was not now, nor could it ever be, anything like heaven to me. I missed my family! Sometimes I wonder why he put up with my childish ways. Here I was about to deliver a child of my own very soon, but all I could think about was how homesick I was.

As the days and weeks rolled by, that little church group became a sort of second family to me. They loved us unconditionally and made sure that we did not spend holidays alone. They stopped by with offerings of food and fun at just the times we needed friends the most. At my lowest moments, someone from the church always called me. When our daughter was born, the Nazarene ladies threw us a baby shower that can only be described as the "mother of all baby showers." We had clothing and accessories to outfit our little baby girl from birth through her first days of kindergarten—all received at one shower! In short, the people of this church loved us with the amazing, unselfish love of Jesus.

Our days on Whidbey Island finally drew to a close. My husband's attack squadron was being sent aboard the USS Midway to the waters off the coast of Vietnam. It was determined that the best thing for me would be to take baby Sonya and go back to Ohio and stay with my family during his nine-month deployment. I'll never forget the last Sunday evening we attended the little Nazarene church. The song leader asked if anyone had a favorite song they wanted to sing and said that we should state the reason it was our favorite. With tears running down my face, I raised my hand and asked them to sing "This Is Like Heaven to Me." My voice faltered as I said, "It wasn't my favorite song in the beginning because I wouldn't let it be! But now, I feel like I am leaving a part of heaven to go back to Ohio."

Like the Israelites, I had originally chosen not to sing the Lord's song in a strange land. But, thankfully, God continued to work in my life. In the end, I was more like a goldfinch who was singing because God wanted me to.

As I watch the roller-coaster flight pattern of the goldfinches, I am amazed at how they can sing when their way is so bumpy. And I am carried back in my memory to roller coaster rides of my own. My dad's factory held a picnic for its employees every year at a now-defunct small amusement park called "Russell's Point" on Indian Lake in Ohio. I remember Dad taking me by the hand at the Westinghouse family picnic when I was a little girl and saying, "C'mon, Raelene—we are going to ride the roller coaster." It was a wooden roller coaster, rather small in comparison to the wild rides offered at large amusement parks today. But it was very scary to me, and I was not at all sure I wanted to ride it. He assured me that I would love it. Sure enough, when the ride ended and I caught the breath that had left me on that first interminably long drop, I begged, "Can we go again?!"

Many years later we took our own children to Kings Island, and it was time for our son's first roller coaster ride. In the children's section of the park was a small coaster called "The Beastie." Kyer was none too sure he wanted to ride it and was near tears as we climbed aboard. But halfway through, he yelled, "This is fun! Can we go again?"

Sometimes life is like a big roller coaster ride. We look at the size of the hills and the twists and turns and are not at all sure we can do it. It is then that I am reminded of the flight pattern of the goldfinches. I wonder if perhaps it is because their way is bumpy that they have learned how to sing through it all.

As we watch the little gold birds hang upside down to eat, or as I think of Dicky nibbling the leaf I put into his cage, I am reminded that God has promised to care for all our needs. I pray that some day I will learn the wisdom of these birds, so that whether I am "molting" in order to grow new feathers, or hanging upside down to avoid other mean birds as I eat, or just riding the roller coaster of life, I will always remember to sing praises to the Lord.

## Chapter Two

# *Parakeets*

At the same time that we had Dicky, the canary, I got personally acquainted with a parakeet that belonged to my maternal grandparents. Mom tells me that Grandma chose Chee Chee's name from a favorite character on a radio soap opera. Evidently Grandma really loved the character, for she had given this name to more than one bird friend. In fact, before I knew the word "parakeet," I thought that the name for that species was "Chee Chee bird."

Grandma's Chee Chee was tame and very loved. I can remember Chee Chee sitting on the edge of the table while we ate at Grandma's house. My grandparents would give Chee Chee tiny bites of their food and laugh as he ate people food.

Chee Chee was not in his cage very often—only at night, in fact. The rest of the time he had complete freedom to go wherever he wanted at Grandma's house. But almost always he loved to simply ride around on Grandma's shoulder. This penchant of his to ride on her shoulder led to some sadness for my somewhat confused, aging grandmother one day when she walked outside with her friend sitting in his usual spot. Of course, the inevitable happened—Chee Chee took off like a proverbial "bird out of its cage."

I remember Grandma crying and saying, "He is too tame! He'll never make it in the wild world. Probably a cat will have him for lunch." Not easily daunted, however, Grandma purchased another Chee Chee. She must have had a real way with birds, for this Chee Chee also was quite tame. Before I was five years old, I knew how to move my index finger ever so slowly toward the bird's perch and rub his belly. Chee Chee II would ride on my finger, my shoulder or even my head (but that hurt when he tried to curl his feet into my hair). Sadly, this Chee Chee also flew off Grandma's shoulder when she walked out onto the porch to water her flowers. I often wondered where the birds flew off to.

## Bimbo Joins the Family

Shortly after this incident, a wonderful, little parakeet came to live at our house. Like both of the Chee Chees, he was green and yellow. We dubbed him "Bimbo"—I think the name came from a nonsense song Mom had picked up from some radio commercial. For she would hold the new bird

11

perched on her right index finger and cup her other hand around his back to make him feel secure as she sang,

Bimbo Bimbo, where you gonna go-lee-o?
Bimbo Bimbo what you gonna do-lee-o?
Bimbo Bimbo, does your mommy know?
You're goin' down the road to see your little girl-lee-o!

Bimbo was a happy little playmate for me when my brothers were in school. He sat on my shoulder a lot. When the weather was nice, I remember Mom warning me never to go outside with him perched on my shoulder—and there would be a sad, faraway look in her eyes as she said it.

We had a rather large, two-story house. Bimbo could fly well, and sometimes even made it upstairs. It was hard to shoo him back downstairs, so Mom eventually clipped his wings. I am not sure how this process works. I don't know if it was painful for the bird or if it is just like a haircut for us, but Bimbo was much more manageable, tame, and friendly afterwards.

However, now there was a new problem—Mom had mistakenly clipped his wings too short! He could not fly up to his cage, which sat on a table near the window in our dining room. We constantly had to pick him up and put him into his cage. Until, that is, my ingenious mother came up with a plan. She and Dad fashioned a ladder out of heavy string, which hung from the door of Bimbo's cage to the floor. My intelligent bird only needed to be placed on the bottom rung of this string ladder one time. He took it from there, pulling himself up with his beak one step at a time until he was back in the safety of his cage. And when I say "safety," Bimbo knew that he needed some safety. For you see, along with five kids and two adults, there was another much-loved member of our family—my calico cat, Tammy. When our parakeet first arrived, Tammy eyed Bimbo hungrily when he walked around on the floor, rode on my shoulder, or sat on someone's finger as he was coaxed to talk. She was reprimanded strongly the first and only time she began to stalk Bimbo—and from then on, she just ignored him. Somehow Tammy understood that even though it seemed very unnatural to her, this green budgie was not meant to be her breakfast.

Bimbo could never carry on a conversation with you, but he certainly mastered two words. Anyone could understand when he would say, "Pretty Bimbo." He definitely did not suffer from low self-esteem. A complete stranger could approach his cage and ask, "What's the bird's name?" only to have this tiny green bird reply, "Pretty Bimbo." Many a guest in our home was surprised and delighted by his response.

The books in the pet shop about training birds tell you to place a mirror in their cage, along with a swing and food and water cups. The idea is that the mirror will make the bird think there is another bird in the cage, and they can play together. Bimbo had a mirror in his cage, but eventually it had to be removed because he thought it was his child. He would take a mouthful of seed and then try to feed it to the bird in the mirror. What a wonderful father he would have been! However, the mirror had to come out when he began to lose weight and grow weak because he was giving all his food to the other bird—the one in the mirror.

Suddenly the day came when Bimbo's health began to fail at an alarming rate. We were never sure what the disease was that caused Bimbo to begin to lose his balance and fall off his perch. Mom tried every remedy the pet store owner suggested, but the bird continued to grow weaker. Mom told me many years later that she just couldn't stand watching him suffer. And so one day, when I came home from school, I was told that Bimbo had died. In reality, he had been dying for some time. One of my cousins had stopped by to visit my mom during the day. When he saw Bimbo's plight, he asked how she could stand to let the little bird suffer. When she explained that she had tried every known remedy to help Bimbo, my cousin told her to give him a paper sack. None of us is exactly sure what happened at that point...but Bimbo was no longer suffering.

I suppose there were tears on my part. I know there were tears on my mom's part. I wondered if she was thinking of the two recently departed Chee Chees? All I can remember is the warm embrace of a woman who knew that a little girl would miss her Bimbo, and how our tears mingled together that day.

## Bambi Arrives

Many years later, I was a young mother myself. Remembering the fun I had had with Bimbo, I decided to get a pet bird for my children. He was a gorgeous white parakeet. Wanting a name that a bird could say as clearly as my Bimbo had repeated his own, I named him "Bambi." Bambi was a fun diversion for our children and had a special love of sitting on our son's head while he watched TV. Kyer's head was always ticklish, and he would giggle as Bambi nuzzled him gently.

Like my mom had done with Bimbo, we allowed Bambi freedom inside our home. Bambi soon developed a particular love of taking a shower. And, so, whenever I was doing dishes, he would squawk to be let out of his cage. When the dishes were done, we would allow a trickle of water to run in the sink and open the door to Bambi's cage. He flew like a B-47 on a mission directly to the sink and frolicked in his own personal shower for several minutes while I had fun watching him.

Bambi never learned to say his name. In fact, as Bambi grew he didn't have much personality, other than the love of showers. As time went on, he seemed to get wilder rather than tamer. He avoided the kids, and mostly spent his time squawking and squawking. We moved his cage as far away from the television as possible, but even when he was allowed to fly free, his continued squawking began to slowly drive us crazy. That is why Bambi eventually went to live in a new home. Perhaps the new owners were able to tame him a bit more, or perhaps they got him a bird friend to keep his squawking down to a dull roar. By the time we gave him away, we were all so weary of his voice that, sad to say, none of us even missed him.

## Desire to be Free

When I remember the Chee Chees and their flights to freedom or Bimbo's clipped wings or Bambi's incessant squawking, I realize that pet birds all have an inborn desire to be free. In that way they are not so different from human beings. My favorite period of history to read, study, and write about is the time just before the Civil War, when so many brave Americans were involved in the intrigue and mystery associated with the "Underground Railroad." The slaves of the South were aided in their escape northward by people who defied what was then the law of the land because they felt they were obeying a higher law. I think the first report I ever wrote was in the third grade about a book called *A Lantern in the Window.* The book related stories about the Underground Railroad, and I have been hooked on learning about it ever since.

Perhaps one of the bravest women who ever lived was Harriet Tubman. She was born in 1820 as a slave. She escaped to the North in 1849, after overhearing that her master was intending to sell some of his slaves to the Deep South. But she was not content to be free herself. She made 19 trips back to the South to help her family and friends escape. There are documented records showing that Ms. Tubman helped over 300 people find freedom.

In 1842, Mary Shindler wrote a beautiful spiritual song which was often heard by the escaping slaves as they stayed in the "stations" of the "underground railroad." Based on Psalm 11:1, the opening lyrics instruct the struggling person to "flee as a bird to your mountain." It must have encouraged the people to keep going until they reached the freedom to be found in Canada. This hymn could also be a theme song for my husband. When the trials of life in general and the burdens of being a pastor begin to overwhelm him, Dan's desire is always to flee to the freedom of the Great Smoky Mountains. Somehow looking at those lofty heights helps him to refocus and to remember the words of John 8:36, "If the Son therefore shall make you free, ye shall be free indeed." When we return from a trip to the mountains, we are better able to enjoy our inner spiritual freedom which is, of course, the most important kind.

My mother is a lover of nursery rhymes. She used to recite them for my brothers and me. Then, 20 years later, she did the same thing with my children. One of her favorites was to hold up her two index fingers and say:

"Two little birds, sitting on a hill—one named Jack and one named Jill,

"Fly away Jack (at this point she would put her left hand behind her back),

"Fly away Jill (now her right hand would be hidden).

"Come back Jack (her left hand with the wiggling index finger returned),

"Come back Jill" (and at last her right hand came back into view—including the wiggling index finger which had been magically transformed in the child's mind to a bird).

Invariably when Mom would play this little game with my children, they would giggle and say, "Do it again, Grandma!" She tells me that she had learned the little rhyming game from her own mother.

My earliest memories of birds in general and of parakeets in particular are all tied up with memories of Grandma and Mom in my mind. Mom taught us that, like the little birds Jack and Jill from the nursery rhyme, we were free to fly away; but that we were always more than welcome to come back, as well. For that knowledge I am eternally grateful.

## Chapter Three

# *Hummingbirds*

*W*hen I was a child, I was often referred to as the "baby of the family." In fact, to this day some of my brothers introduce me as their "baby sister." I suppose this would bother some people, but to me it has always sounded like a term of endearment. I don't ever remember wishing that I was the older child or that I had a younger sibling. While I would have loved to have had a sister, I think in my mind's eye it was always an older sister that I longed for and not a younger one. You see, I think I always liked the special attention and the extra care given to me as the family's baby.

As I speak to other people, I find that I am not alone in this. To enjoy being the baby of the clan has even been portrayed on television in one of my all-time favorite programs, "The Waltons." My kids used to watch that program and laugh at how the baby of the family, Elizabeth, was often sitting on someone's lap (usually her father's) or being hauled around by a brother or sister when she appeared to be much too old to be carried. Her relationship with her older siblings often mirrored my own. She was babied, petted, and thoroughly enjoyed by all. While I was never favored as much as it appeared Miss Elizabeth was, I always did feel especially loved by my parents and brothers. For this reason, I have always been interested in small things.

## God's Handiwork

Throughout the Bible, God's love for little things and little people is evident. God's handiwork is never more apparent than it is when you view the tiniest bird of all, and one of my favorites, the hummingbird.

I once had a hummingbird feeder hanging in front of the picture window in our living room, about six inches from the window. The feeder was simply a clear plastic bottle-shaped affair with four little perches and holes that go into the bottle at each perch. We filled it with a mixture of sugar and water and red food coloring, since for some reason, hummingbirds are attracted to the color red. This feeder gave me the fantastic opportunity to study the little birds, up close and personal. They are truly amazing creatures.

Here in Ohio the most common type of "hummer" is the ruby-throated hummingbird. The male of the species has a bright red throat which offsets his iridescent green back and wing feathers, making him look like a Christmas bird. The female is all green in color, but equally beautiful. The feathers have such a luminous quality that in the early 1800s, women used them to make jewelry and decorative additions to their clothing. Indeed, having the entire little bird (stuffed, of course) on a lady's hat was considered a mark of distinction. Sadly, the population of hummingbirds was so depleted by this practice that some species became extinct as a result.

Magical is the word that best describes the movements of a hummingbird. It is the only bird that can fly backwards or straight up and down while its body remains horizontal, or hover in mid-air. I loved to stand back a few feet from my window (remaining in the shadows) and watch a little guy come to the feeder. It resembled a tiny helicopter as it hovers over the feeder and decides which of the four feeding stations makes the safest perch. If there were other birds nearby, it hovered as it drank the red nectar with its long beak—ever ready to zoom away to safety. If it came during a quiet time when no other animals were about, it perched and took long, satisfying draughts before flying with lightning speed back to the top branches of the tree, where it undoubtedly had a nest. I have read about the biological reasons why the hummingbird can fly so differently from all other species of birds. What it boils down to, in my mind at least, is that God created this petite little creature with lots of special abilities because it is so small. Our wonderful Creator proves through the existence of this bird that, once again, He loves and cares for the very smallest elements of our society.

There have been a few documented cases of large insects being able to overcome and destroy a hummingbird, and the remains of the darling little shining creatures have been found caught in some spiders' webs. But when the bird only weighs as much as a penny, I suppose it is no wonder that a few of them fall prey to disaster. For the most part, though, a healthy hummingbird can outmaneuver any potential enemy with its amazing abilities to fly in any direction at jet-like speed.

Hummers' eating habits are exhausting to watch. Studies have shown that the average food requirement for a hummingbird is between two and four grams per day. Of course, that seems miniscule to us, but in human terms, that means the average man would have to eat over 300 pounds of food each day to keep up with the bird! Knowing this makes it even more interesting to observe how much energy the little bird expends with his flight. The wings beat so rapidly that the naked eye cannot observe their movement, but we can certainly hear their hum. In fact, many times when I was on our porch, I instinctively dove for cover from what I thought was a bumblebee or a wasp, only to discover that it was an innocent little hummingbird.

The hummingbirds came to the feeder at about 15-minute intervals throughout the day. (I wonder what I would look like if I were to eat every 15 minutes.) They drink deeply with their beak, which measures approximately one-fifth of their total body length, from the nectar of many flowers. Of course, the nectar in the feeder is not the only food source the birds pursue. They aid in the population control of insects by consuming gnats and mosquitoes, grabbing them with their long, fringed tongue mid-flight. Since I really detest those insects, hummingbirds are some of my dearest friends.

I am told that the hummingbird's nest is not much bigger than a walnut and is attached to a branch high in a tree. The mother bird lays two eggs at a time, each of which is only one-half inch long. The nest is constructed in such a way that the top edge turns inward, protecting the tiny eggs from being tossed out of their warm home in a windstorm. How amazing that the time between when the babies are hatched until their first, long migratory flight to the warm mountains of Central America, is only a few months. Patient feeding every quarter hour by Mrs. Hummingbird allows them to achieve adulthood and the ability to "hum" their way southward in record time. This is one more proof that God cares deeply about the miniscule birds.

## Going to the Altar

I think the first time that I was really aware of how God cares for small people, as well as small birds, came when I was five years old. Though our church had a nursery and a toddler room, from the time a child was about four they were trained to sit in adult church quietly. In the churches that my husband has pastored, sometimes parents pride themselves on their child's ability to sit in church—but rarely is the child quiet throughout the service. More often than not, the kids are kicking the pews in front of them or arguing audibly with the parent that they are "bored" and "want to go home."

Mom tells the story that one time when I was a toddler, I was acting up during the service. She picked me up and carried me to the basement; I was ecstatic, thinking I was going to the nursery and could play with the toys. Instead of the nursery, however, we entered the ladies room, where Mom applied her hand to my backside and told me that I was to sit quietly during the rest of the service. As soon as I regained my composure, which was amazingly fast with a mother who would threaten that I should stop crying or she would "give me something to cry about," we went back upstairs. She says that from that day forward, whenever I was being ornery in the worship service she would simply ask, "Do you want to go to the basement?" and I would straighten up and fly right.

So week after week I would sit in the pew beside my Mom, looking for all the world like I was busy coloring my Sunday School paper, but the pastor's sermons were actually pricking my sinful, little five-year-old heart. When the invitation was given one week to come to the altar to accept Christ as Savior, I walked down the aisle by myself and knelt to pray. Mom tells me that as I started down the aisle, the pastor said, "And a little child shall lead them." Of course he was taking the passage from Isaiah 11:6 (which is talking about the millennial kingdom) out of context. No one seemed to care, though.

I must have looked very little as I approached the altar that day. Some would say I was too young to know what I was doing. I remember, however, that my big brother Bob came from the choir loft and knelt beside me. He opened his Bible to John 3:16 and replaced each of the "whosoevers" with the name "Raelene," gently explaining and asking me questions to make sure that I understood before we prayed together and I asked Jesus to come into my heart. The Lord met me there and welcomed me into His kingdom. Is it any wonder, then, that I am impressed with God's care of "little things," since I was so little when He forgave me and made me His own child!

## An Easter Hummingbird

In the congregation where my husband recently served

as pastor, we had a darling little "hummingbird." Her name is Montanna. She is the "almost six-year-old" daughter of our youth directors. My husband describes her as being "five going on 15," for she is very mature for her age. In fact, she always has been. I don't think I have ever known a child who so obviously had been given a particular spiritual gift before Montanna came into our lives. Ever since she was a tiny baby, she has been a source of encouragement to all who come her way.

I will never forget Easter Sunday morning a few years ago. Easter had always been a big deal in my family. We colored eggs and decorated the house. We had new clothes for the day. And the "Easter Bunny" had always magically come sometime during the night before Easter, leaving baskets of wonderful candy for us kids. (I know there are those who think such practices are sinful, and that they confuse children as to the true meaning of the holiday, but this was never a problem in our home. We always knew that what we were celebrating was the fact that Jesus rose from the dead on this day. But along with the spiritual significance of Easter, it was a fun holiday in our home.)

Dan and I did the same things for our children as our parents had done for us. Our kids had always looked forward to coloring eggs, and it became a game for Dan to try to get his egg to turn black. He would dip it in each of the different colors, over and over again. The kids would "egg him on," and he usually accomplished having an egg that was at least a dirty gray shade, if not black. So, along with the spiritual significance of the holiday, it had always been a special family day for me.

One year, neither of our grown kids could come home for Easter, and my parents were traveling to be with one of my brothers, so I was having a little private pity party for myself.

In this frame of mind, I played the organ for the sunrise service and endured the breakfast served by our young adults. During the morning worship service, I was still feeling sad because our family was so scattered. I looked around at all the children in their new bonnets and finery, sitting with their parents and their grandparents, and I was jealous. When I made my way back to the pew after the music ended, I stared straight ahead, blinking back tears. Suddenly, I realized a little hand had slipped inside mine.

Little two-and-a-half-year-old Montanna had noticed my distress. She came up to sit beside me and reached for my hand. I wiped away the tears and pulled her up into my lap and hugged her. She leaned back and looked me straight in the face and said, "Don't be sad, Miss Raelene. I love you, and Jesus is alive!" Out of the mouths of babes!

That was not the only time that Montanna has sensed a problem and tried to encourage me. Her mother and grand-mother tell me that she does it all the time at home. Montanna is the tiniest five-year-old you have ever seen. Her younger brother will soon pass her in height and has probably already passed her in weight. But I doubt there has ever been a child that could pass her in being an encourager to those who need it. Like the little hummingbirds, she is tiny but mighty.

And so, as I gaze from the shadows of my living room at the amazing little hummingbird, I am reminded that God cares immensely about little things. I am so glad that He cared so much for a little redheaded girl in 1955 that He entered my life, never to leave. And I am thankful for a darling little girl in our congregation who can sense when I need a hug.

Last summer we only saw one pair of hummers at our feeder. I named the ruby-throated male Zaccheus, for he was indeed a wee little "man" for whom the Lord cared deeply. I prayed that as I watched him, I would remember to always remain little (humble) in my own eyes, as we are instructed in God's Word. And I prayed that, like little Montanna, I would be a source of encouragement to the people the Lord puts in my life each day.

Chapter Four

# *Blue Jays & Nuthatches*

uring the same camping vacations when my mother was so enamored with the goldfinches (or "wild canaries," as she called them), I liked to watch for blue jays. By the time I had reached high school, my brothers were all grown, so Mom and Dad allowed me to take a friend along on our trips to Gun Lake. My best pal from school, Nancy, went along. Mom would talk about the lovely, little yellow birds, but Nancy and I would say that we preferred the big blue jays. As only teenagers can do, we dismissed the lovely song of the finches and claimed that the jays were cool because they were bigger and louder and feistier. Mom said that the jays were not only feisty, they were mean! I remember shaking my head and rolling my eyes (behind Mom's back, of course), and saying how pretty the blue jays were. Of course, Mom agreed that they were beautiful birds, with their striking blue feathers and that fancy topknot, but she did not like them. Now that I have grown up, I tend to agree with her. Blue jays are beautiful, but they are definitely mean. Nancy is in heaven now, having succumbed to cancer when she was much too young to die, but I am sure she would agree that what Mom said back then is true: "Beauty is as beauty does."

Blue jays may be gorgeous birds, but to backyard bird-watchers like me, their actions destroy that beauty. They don't seem to have any song, except their raucous scream of "jay jay." They are so much larger than the other birds at my feeder that the others fly away in fear each time they approach. I find myself wanting to say, "Get away, you bullies! Let the little birds get the seed. Go find your own food." If some little bird is tenacious enough to hold his post when the larger, noisier bird arrives, the blue jay is likely to nip at the smaller bird until it abandons the feeder also. Mean is the only word that fits Mr. Blue Jay.

## The Nuthatch

Another strange little bird, called a nuthatch, is much the same as the blue jay. Mr. Nuthatch is shaped differently than most other birds. It looks like his head is joined directly to the rest of his body, with no neck in between. Indeed, it appears that his head takes up half of his little body. He is bluish-gray and white and his markings are strikingly beautiful. He has a black cap on his head and a rather long beak for his short, stubby body. He is quite an acrobat, since he often can be seen climbing down a tree or post head-first. These birds eat insects gleaned from the bark of trees. Why, then, do they come so often and scare the other birds away from my feeder? I believe it is for sheer orneriness' sake alone. When the nuthatch arrives, it is just like when a blue jay comes—all the other little song-birds abandon ship. Unlike the noisy blue jay, however, the nuthatch is capable of producing a pretty song. But he seems to favor screaming a bass-sounding "yank yank" rather than singing. All the better for scaring away the other birds, I believe.

Whenever a blue jay or a nuthatch arrives at a feeder, the other birds seem to visibly cower in fear. And no wonder! I have seen both of these birds reach out and nip at the tail or wing of another species. If that doesn't do the trick, they will actually attack the other bird. I have watched many fights at my feeder, and it seems the perpe-trator of every one has always been either a blue jay or a nuthatch. If I had my way, these two types of birds would be banished not only from my yard, but from all yards where other birds seem to be able to live in harmony!

As I watch the jays and the nuthatches, I am often re-minded of people who seem to make it their goal in life to pick at other people and to destroy the harmony that should exist in a church. If you have been in a church or any other social organization for very long, you know that there are certain people who tend to cause trouble wherever they go. It's bad enough when it happens in a PTA or other group that meets for social reasons alone, but when there is someone in a church group causing unrest and disharmony at every opportunity, it seems doubly bad. And yet, like the blue jays and the nuthatches, they come.

## The Songbirds Get Attacked

In one of our pastorates, there were two dear little ladies who were absolute saints in my book. They were sisters who had both been widowed at an early age. Though they were extremely close and got along well, they lived across the street from each other, each preferring to keep her own home.

Sophie was the younger and the smaller of the two. Her hair was gray, and she was a bit bent from arthritis. Her husband had been a pastor. She had a beautiful soprano voice, and she loved little children. In fact, she ran a day care center for preschoolers in our church building. Though she was "getting up there" in age (or so it seemed to this young pastor's wife at the time), all the children immediately loved her. (Children, I have found, are very good judges of character.) Our own kids were in elementary school at the time. Our daughter was nearly as tall as tiny Sophie, and they were good pals. Sonya could often be found sitting with Sophie during worship services.

Maria was the older sister. Her hair remained quite dark, though I am positive she never colored it. Her voice was a little raspy, but she could often still sing in a strong alto voice. The sisters' duets were wonderful, though we could never convince them to sing in front of the congregation. When I think of Maria, I think of complete peacefulness. If Sophie became a bit agitated over a problem in the church or in their lives, it would always be Maria who would say, "Sister, calm yourself. We know from past experience that God will work this all out for good."

Both sisters made wonderful quilts. In fact, in the four years that we were in that church, I don't ever remember being in either of their houses when there was not a quilt frame dominating the living room. They patiently and lovingly taught me to quilt, and we spent many happy hours together, piecing scraps into lovely patterns.

My husband always thought it was funny that they would each have a quilt going at the same time, because every evening found them both at one or the other of their homes, quilting together. "Why don't they just live together?" Dan would ask. "They eat together every night and spend every evening quilting together. It makes no sense."

Perhaps only a woman could understand that they maintained their individual homes for many reasons. I am sure one of those reasons was that their personalities, while similar in some ways, were still quite different in others. They each preferred to cook and bake and do canning in their own kitchens. No kitchen has ever been made that is big enough for two cooks, even sisters who love each other dearly. Sophie, ever thinking of pleasing the children, was known to make more cookies and sweets. Maria was a bit of a health nut, back before doing so was cool. She shared new ways to use broccoli and asparagus, while her sister brought us yummy red raspberry pies. I told Dan not to try to talk them into moving in together, even though financially it would have been easier for them. He did not understand, but I did.

Sophie and Maria always reminded me of the Baldwin sisters on the television program "The Waltons." Of course, my friends did not spend their time making the "Recipe" (the Baldwins' code word for moonshine whiskey), but Sophie and Maria had many of the same mannerisms as the sisters on the TV program. They shared many wonderful recipes with me—for things like cornmeal quiche and pickled carrots and no-bake fruit pies made with jello and cornstarch. Perhaps the most important way they seemed to resemble the Baldwins was in their constant love for, and deep devotion to, each other. Just as the Baldwins were wonderful friends to the Waltons, so were Sophie and Maria wonderful friends to their pastor's family. We knew that they were our strongest supporters and closest confidants. In short, these ladies were godly.

Why, then, did other people in the church pick at them so unmercifully? If they were jealous of our close relationship with the sisters, why didn't they understand that even the pastor's wife needed friends? Why did people misjudge everything Sophie and Maria did? Although the congregation elected them year after year to the church board, they continued to accuse them of "running the church." People said that Sophie should step down from teaching the children in Sunday School, but refused to get involved in teaching themselves. When the sisters gave a sizeable amount of money to have the bell from the original building placed in a special little stand in a flower garden at the church (memorializing their parents, who had been charter members), people said that it was a self-serving act on their parts. Why did so many in this little congregation treat these dear sisters in the same way that the blue jays and nuthatches treat the little songbirds?

"Pick a little, talk a little, pick a little, talk a little—cheep, cheep, cheep, talk a lot, pick a little more!" These are words from a song in Meredith Wilson's famous movie "The Music Man," starring Robert Preston and Shirley Jones. In the movie, the song is about the ladies of the town who gossip and misjudge each other all the time. The women just pick at each other and tear each other's reputations to bits. I think of it every time I see a blue jay or a nuthatch. I am transported back in time to that pastorate, where two godly women were picked at and talked about unmercifully. Yet, like the little songbirds who come back to my feeder when the nasty birds fly away, Sophie and Maria patiently bore the abuse without ever fighting back! What pictures of God's grace they were to a young, impressionable pastor's wife!

In Proverbs 6, Solomon lists six things that the Lord hates, stating that "seven are an abomination unto Him." The seventh thing on the list (the straw that breaks the camel's back) is "he who sows discord among the brethren."

I think there have always been blue jays and nuthatches in every church congregation. There have always been those who like to gossip. Every pastor on the face of the earth could recount horror stories. We were warned to give a wide berth to people who want to tell you about all the problems with the former pastor and found this to be very wise counsel.

## Our Experience With Blue Jays

The man who met us at the door at one of the churches we served seemed to love us immediately. He was the one who took us shopping for a new refrigerator for the parsonage, telling us as we rode to the store, "Now you pick out exactly what you want. Don't worry about the money. This church can afford it. We are so excited to have you as our pastor and wife. We want to get you the very best. You are following a man we did not like, and we are thankful to be rid of him!" He also said he wanted to tell us which church members we should be on the watch for because they were likely to cause us trouble. And this was the first day we lived there!

This man taught the Senior High Sunday School class in that church. We had only been there a few months when the lid blew off that class! Like a good pastor's wife should, I try to never leave Sunday School or church for any reason, but that week I had an inexplicable need to go to the restroom during Sunday School. Embarrassed, I tiptoed out of the classroom and hurried into the ladies' room. Imagine my surprise when I found a young lady in there crying her eyes out. As I entered the room, she nearly knocked me down by hurling herself into my arms. "I can't stay in that class. I won't listen to it another minute. He's wrong!" she sobbed. Within a few minutes, I discovered that our friendly buyer-of-refrigerators man was teaching his Sunday School students that there is absolutely nothing wrong with abortion. Thank the Lord for Emily, who had stood up to him and left the class in disgust.

The next week was chaotic in that congregation. It culminated in a church board meeting where the teacher was relieved of his class. When approached about the subject, he shouted that he did not care what the Bible said in Psalm 139 or about our denomination's stand on the topic. He saw nothing wrong with abortion. As a result of his attitude, he was also asked to resign as a board member and relinquish his church membership. He actually threatened my husband as he left the church that evening, never to return. Dan later told me that in an effort to calm himself down, my husband had picked up a hymnbook and squeezed it tightly with both hands behind his back. By the time the man was walking out of the building, after verbally attacking me, Emily, and others with poisonous words, Dan feared he might actually deck him if his hands weren't occupied with something else.

A couple weeks later, we thought that all the picking and talking and cheeping (not unlike the blue jays and nuthatches) had subsided. Then one day I received a phone call. It was, thankfully, from a songbird and not a blue jay in our congregation. She related how she had heard a horrible rumor about me from various sources. She said, "Raelene, if it is true, I want you to know that I will forgive you and stand beside you—because I know there must have been extenuating circumstances. But if it is not true, I want to help you nip this thing in the bud."

By now, I was petrified. What had she heard? Through tears, she reported that the man who left the church was telling everyone that the reason Dan was so strongly opposed to abortion was because he had discovered that I had aborted a baby! The man who had once seemed like a little nuthatch or the larger blue jay now had become a vulture, circling his prey and coming in for the kill.

I cried and asked why God would allow this to happen so early in this new pastorate. We sought wise counsel from our district superintendent as to what was the best course to take. Since the rumor had become so widespread and there were now so many variations of it floating around the church, he advised Dan to tell his church board that it was completely unfounded—and then go about the business of preaching and never mention it again.

We did this, and that congregation grew to love us. I was thankful for the training I had received at the quilt frames in the homes of Sophie and Maria. I could still hear Maria saying, "Calm yourself, sister. God is in control."

I am thankful that sometimes days and weeks go by when I do not see a blue jay or a nuthatch. Our ministry has also gone for long periods of time without any cheeping or picking at us or among the congregation. I pray that every time I see one of these birds that I do not like, I will be reminded of how God views those who pick at others. For you see, even a pastor's wife can be drawn into cheeping and picking when I should be singing!

Chapter Five

## *Bluebirds*

*W*hen I began going to school, I found out early on that I was a good student. The first indication of this came in first grade, when the students in the class were divided into reading groups. Of course the teacher tried her best to play down the fact that one group of readers was quicker than the other one. But when, in just a few weeks, the Bluebirds were a book ahead of the Redbirds—we all knew! Basically, if you were a Bluebird you were pretty smart, and I fear we were pretty cocky in our little first grade way. The Redbirds were just a little slow and struggled. Sometimes a lucky child was moved from the Redbirds into the Bluebirds group—what a happy day that was for him! But woe to the poor child who was told in a stage whisper by Mrs. Hughes, "I think it would be good for you to become a Redbird for awhile." All of this reminiscing makes me wonder if it was in first grade that I decided that blue was my favorite color. Indeed, I have to be careful or my entire wardrobe would be blue, and the main color of my living room furniture is blue. Could it be because I was labeled a "Bluebird" by Mrs. Hughes? As an adult, I have learned to admire the little eastern bluebird for its own sake. For in many ways, it seems to be an emissary from God to our sad, sinful world.

Before my mother began to lose her eyesight, one of her chief joys in life was bird-watching. She was never into it big-time, but she certainly enjoyed looking for all the different species of birds at the feeders near her windows. In the early 1990s, several years after my father's death, she was living with her new husband in his home in the country. Like me, Mom prefers living in town. She was lonely and there were many adjustments to make in her recent marriage. On a particularly sad day, when she felt rather abandoned and frankly was wondering what she had gotten herself into, she sat by a window in their living room fighting tears. Suddenly she heard a different songbird than any she had heard before. She turned her head and saw a beautiful bluebird seated on the ledge just outside the window. Later that day she telephoned me and said, "God sent me a messenger today to let me know that He still loves me and that everything is eventually going to be all right with your stepdad and me." (It has worked out well. They have now been married 15 years.)

Some would say that Mom was exaggerating by claiming that God had sent the lovely little bird. However, I believe that God can do anything. And since He has perfect control over all nature, why couldn't He choose to send a bird to the window to cheer up a sad woman? If the normal habits of a bluebird are studied, it would seem that the little songster Mom saw that day was indeed a special envoy from the Almighty. For bluebirds do not normally get that close to homes or to any signs of human life. They choose, rather, to stay near fence rows and on the edge of fields. I believe, like my mother, that God knew the sight of a bluebird in the midst of that otherwise dark day would cheer His weary daughter in a way that perhaps nothing else could. What an awesome God we serve!

Due to the overpopulation of their natural enemy, the starlings, bluebirds have become so rare that not many people have ever had the opportunity to see one in the wild. A few years back, a woman came to our door and asked if she could have permission to place a "bluebird box" in the expanse of yard just to the west of the parsonage we lived in at the time. She also wanted permission to place a box in the back of the cemetery across the road. Her goal, it seemed, was to reclaim the eastern bluebird for our area by giving them places to nest. These boxes are very precisely built, with a one-and-one-half-inch hole to enter (which discourages the larger starlings), no perch (which would attract wrens), and a slanted roof with an overhang to facilitate drainage. This thoughtful lady and her husband have blanketed the area with the boxes, most of which have been happily inhabited by the rare birds. Her efforts have paid off, and we are eternally grateful. Like my mother, I am often cheered by the sight of these brilliantly colored birds. Watching their habits and listening to their songs have enriched my life in a way that few other birds ever have.

## Mates for Life

Ornithologists tell us that Mr. and Mrs. Bluebird mate for life. They raise family after family of young chicks in the same nest. Daddy bird sings to Mama and brings her little gifts before she lays eggs. After eggs appear in the nest, he can often be seen sitting with her during the incubation period, which averages about 12 days, as if to say, "I'm in this for the long haul. I know you must be bored sitting still for such a long time. I'll stay by your side and protect you from the starlings and keep you company while we wait for our blessed event."

As the young birds begin to hatch, Mother and Father bird swoop into action. They feed the baby birds about every seven minutes, bringing them such delicacies as grasshoppers, crickets, worms, grubs, and berries. This frantic feeding schedule continues through the daylight hours for about three weeks, until the young birds are ready to fly. At this point, Daddy bird takes over the care of the young, and Mama bird cleans and repairs the nest in an effort to ready it for her next brood of four to six eggs. This cycle continues over and over.

God knows that the bluebird is naturally a "neat freak." Knowing in advance that these little birds would reuse the same nest over and over, he built into the baby bird a very unique feature, almost unknown to the rest of the bird kingdom. The excrement from the baby birds comes neatly enclosed in tough little sacs. The male bird can often be seen emerging from the nesting box (or hollow tree or log) carrying one of these fecal sacs in his beak. He drops it outside the nest area where it becomes a part of the earth again, thus helping his wife keep their home neat and clean.

When the nest has been repaired and cleaned after a

brood of chicks has been raised to "flight stage," and Mama begins the cycle again, the young birds help feed their freshly hatched brothers and sisters. They also are taught to help keep the nest area clean. It is easy to imagine that these birds are learning, at the feet of their parents, what family life is all about.

As I watch for the bluebirds who occupy the boxes near our home, I am often disappointed that they do not venture to my bird feeders. In fact, it is rare that one can get a good glimpse of them without binoculars. Bluebirds are truly homebodies, and even the daddy bird does not venture very far from his nest. I truly wish that everyone could get a brief glimpse into the lives of these colorful birds. The lessons they quietly teach are so desperately needed in 21st century America.

## Parenthood Today

The beginning of each school year brings lots of heartache and stress to several elementary school teachers that I know. They have each been teaching for more than 30 years and find themselves comparing the families of today with those of days gone by. Last year one of my friends, who teaches kindergarten, confided to me that she asked the children how many of them lived with their biological mother and father. None of the 26 children in her class could claim that privilege! I commented that when I was in kindergarten, I would not even have known the meaning of the word "biological." The streetwise children of today seem to grow up all too soon, as they make the endless treks between their biological mother and stepdad's home and that of their biological father and stepmom. Of course, perhaps those children are the lucky ones in today's society. Many other children are being raised by their grandparents because their parents do not care what happens to them. And then there are those who live with Daddy and his girlfriend, or the opposite combination. A few are being raised by two mommies or two daddies. Is it any wonder that my teacher friends battle depression as they see how society continues to change and promote more sinful lifestyles each year? If only people could view the mating habits of the beautiful, little eastern bluebirds. Watching them gives new meaning to the word commitment. It doesn't seem to matter to Mr. Bluebird when another bird with more attractive feathers moves into the next bluebird box. He sticks with his mate through thick and thin.

In our last pastorate we were very privileged to have many young couples. Some of them were beginning to raise families. What a joy it was to watch how fatherhood has improved over the years. These young daddies in our church were willing to change diapers, give bottles, wipe noses, and more. In fact, they were much more involved than I remember the men of my own generation ever being. Even when the couples were waiting for the arrival of their babies, these men were like the songbirds who stayed at home and encouraged their wives through the rough days, rather than running hither and yon to play softball or other sports "with the boys," as expectant fathers of my generation were known to do. It would seem that like Papa Bluebird, they realized that this homemaking business is not just for the women folk. When I saw one of the guys carrying a dirty diaper to the trash can, I was reminded of how the bird helps his mate to keep their nest clean by removing the strange fecal sacs. And as the young moms told me of the trials of getting their toddlers to pick up their toys, I was reminded of Mrs. Bluebird cleaning her nest.

This is one trait that I fear we overemphasized with our own kids. Our daughter became such a "neat freak" that our friends and relatives looked askance at us. One time some friends were visiting us when Sonya was only four years old. It was one of those times when the guests did not seem to realize they should take their own four children home at a reasonable hour. Our kids were very sleepy and getting rather grumpy, so we decided that we would go ahead and put them to bed. Sonya cried that she did not want to go to bed. But it was not because she did not want to miss playing with her little friends. It was because her room was messy from the visiting children! To this day, she is an impeccable housekeeper.

This neatness is a trait that she inherited directly from her father. Dan, like Mr. Bluebird, wants his nest to be neat and clean at all times. In fact, he has bypassed third base in this fetish to be neat and often runs full throttle toward home plate over the tiniest infraction of the rules. Early in our marriage, we had a desk in our living room where I would write letters, pay bills, and display knickknacks. I began to notice that the first thing Dan did as he entered our home each evening was to straighten up the desk. To his credit, he never scolded me for leaving the desk in disarray but just quietly cleaned it up himself.

One day I decided to make a game of it. He has always believed that there should be a place for everything and everything should be in that place. Consequently, each time he straightened up the desk, every item would be placed in a particular spot. So while he was at work, I moved one thing to a different place. Sure enough, as he walked through the living room to change out of his Navy uniform into civilian clothing, he put the misplaced item back in its original spot. This went on for at least a month before he caught me laughing at him one afternoon. While I suppose living with Mr. Neatness himself would drive some people crazy, like Mrs. Bluebird I appreciate all the help he gives me around our nest.

Mama Bluebird is rarely ever seen away from her nest, especially once she is raising a brood of chicks. How smart she is! Why do women of today feel that they must gain their identity as a woman by working outside the home? Many claim that they need the extra income, but studies have shown that if a woman is content to be a "keeper of the nest," the added income is usually not needed, since the extra car and money spent for child care consumes so much of her wages. We think we have learned so much since the Industrial Revolution, but a quick glance at the world of the bluebirds convinces me that in many ways we have gone backward rather than forward.

## Bluebird Siblings

Though I have never been able to watch the phenomenon of the very young bluebirds helping to care for their newly hatched brothers and sisters, my research tells me this truly happens. What a reminder of the joy of growing up in a home with siblings who helped to teach me.

I have four older brothers. In fact, the eldest is 15 years older than me! So, by the time I came along, the older ones were going out on dates and living quite a different life from that of their baby sister. However, my brothers have each taught me invaluable lessons. Just like the bluebirds, they helped Mom and Dad to care for their young.

Bill, the oldest (and his dear wife Carolyn), showed me what sacrificial love was all about as I watched them raise their firstborn, Floyd. Floyd was born with hemophilia. When he was small, he was injured so many times as he learned to walk that he was often bruised from head to toe. The rest of the world did not understand about his disease. When our family would go to the beach, you could see people staring at the bruised little boy who was my beloved nephew, just six years younger than me. Bill and Carolyn took the stares and whispers in stride as they tried to allow Floyd to live a normal life. It had to be hard for them as everyone misjudged the cause of his black-and-blue little body, but they held their heads high and smiled with pride over his every accomplishment.

The next bluebird brother is Bob. When I was five years old, he was the one who came down from the church choir during the invitation time and prayed with me, leading me to a certain knowledge that Jesus could love a little girl and come into her heart and life. I will always be thankful that he cared enough to pray with his little sister. Years later, he was the "Youth for Christ" director in our town—at a time when I was a youth. Oh, the good times we had at YFC Club in school and at the biweekly rallies where our club joined with the other area clubs for songs, teaching, fellowship, and fun! I learned a lot about Jesus at the feet of brother Bob. He has always been a spiritual mentor to me, and I am thankful for his godly influence on his baby sister.

Johnny is seven years older than I am. My mother has always attributed the fact that my brother David and I did very well in school to some training we received at brother Johnny's feet. You see, when Johnny was in about fourth grade, my parents decided to lay hardwood flooring in the entire upstairs of our big house. Mom, Dad, Bill, and Bob worked every evening from suppertime until bedtime, measuring boards and pounding nails. To keep the "little kids" occupied, Johnny played school with David and me. I suspect that what he was actually doing was teaching us his own homework each evening. As a direct result of all those hours spent in the kitchen, facing the chalkboard that hung on the pantry door, David and I could both read and do simple math before we ever attended kindergarten. Had Johnny been a bluebird, his little siblings would likely have been flying long before their time!

David is two and one-half years my senior. He taught me some valuable lessons, such as when to duck when playing "Andy Andy Over" with a rock on the garage roof. (A trip to the emergency room for stitches is a valuable learning tool.) He also taught me where to place my feet when I sat on the handlebars of his bike for a ride. He played hours and hours of board games with his little sister. (I learned from him that the person who purchases all the railroads almost invariably wins the game of Monopoly.)

I think at one time or another every one of my brothers tried to teach me to drive. Considering that I am a reasonably intelligent person, this task was ridiculously hard for me to learn. The coordination required to step on the pedals and turn the steering wheel at the same time seemed to have bypassed me. In time, my dad was the patient Mr. Bluebird who conquered the nearly insurmountable feat, and I passed the State of Ohio driving test with flying colors at age 19!

I don't know if bluebird children also teach their siblings as they help feed them. I do know that whenever I see a young bluebird, I am reminded to be thankful for the four boys who teased me unmercifully but loved me unconditionally and stood up for me when I needed it.

# Bluebirds

I fear that too many 21st century American children have never known the love of a tight-knit family such as the bluebird enjoys. The Bible gives such clear-cut blueprints for how to make a family work in chapters five and six of Ephesians. Why are we so slow to learn? Why can't we be more like the seemingly simple little creatures called bluebirds?

When I was a young child, I often heard Mom and Dad singing a famous song from World War II in beautiful harmony. The only words I remember were, "There'll be bluebirds over the white cliffs of Dover tomorrow.... Just you wait and see." When I asked Dad what the song was about, he explained that during the War, the skies above Europe were so full of planes dropping bombs and having dogfights in the sky that the bluebirds all seemed to disappear. And so, it was a song of hope—that someday the fighting would stop and the bluebirds would again be seen flying over the beautiful white cliffs of Dover, England. I haven't heard the song in years. But every sighting of a bluebird is a sign of hope that people will learn to live in harmonious family units again, where Mother, Father, and children of all ages can sing praises to the One who first conceived the idea of family in Genesis chapter one, and who still believes in it today.

Chapter Six

## *Cardinals*

If anyone ever doubted the existence of God or His wonderful creative powers, all they would have to do to be convinced of both is to view a pair of cardinals. Perhaps more than any other bird, a cardinal makes his heavenly Creator "look good." Whenever a group of people is asked to name their favorite bird, someone is bound to say it is the cardinal. According to the Audubon Society, cardinals have been chosen as the official state bird by more states than any other bird. Illinois, Indiana, Kentucky, Ohio, West Virginia, and North Carolina all honor the beautiful red bird.

One reason many people like cardinals is because, unlike other types of birds, the female is almost as strikingly beautiful as the male. Although the male is the bright red one, his wife is just a little duller shade of red, mixed with a bit of brown. This color combination gives her almost an orange hue. Both the males and females have wonderful crests atop their heads, and their eyes stand out with a gorgeous, smoky ring that resembles mascara. Even their beaks are bright red or orange and have a conical shape which distinguishes them from many other species and adds to their dramatic appearance. Nothing is more beautiful than the sight of a pair of cardinals set against a stark white backdrop of snow-covered earth. And if the gentle observer of the birds is brave enough to stick his head out a door or open a window in the wintertime, he will find that not only do the cardinals look gorgeous, they sound gorgeous for they sing year round.

I remember one of my earliest attempts at whistling involved trying to mimic the distinct call of the cardinal. I had barely mastered the art of pursing my lips and blowing through them to create a sound when I began to whistle back to a cardinal. Imagine my surprise when Mr. Bird responded to my call. I doubt there is a child alive who has not had a conversation with a cardinal, for their series of slurred whistles is easy to follow and imitate. I wonder, what I have said to these birds down through the years. To this day, whenever I see one, I always whistle their call. I hope the bird knows that I am thanking him for gracing my lawn and allowing me to view him.

It is fun to watch a pair of cardinals at the feeder. We always try to purchase bird food that contains a lot of sunflower seeds and corn, for that is the food that attracts these most colorful of all the birds that live in our area. When they come to the feeder, it is almost invariably a pair of them, traveling life's highways and byways together. One will get some seed in his beak and immediately feed it into the beak of his or her mate. Often they just sit and stare at each other awhile between this ritual, as if to say, "Look at us, world! We are in love! We are beautiful! We were made by a wonderful God who cares about you."

## Serving Others

As I have both observed and researched cardinals, I haven't discovered a single bad habit that they possess. Mating for life, raising their children, caring for each other's needs ahead of their own, and always looking good—now that is an example that each of us should follow! Wouldn't it be neat if we could someday hear God say, "Thank you for always making Me look good"?

When my husband was in the military, he was taught that one of the main goals of the sailor or soldier (he served in both the Navy and the Army) was to make his commanding officer look good. During boot camp days, when the recruits were trained in everything from bed-making to executing a proper salute to keeping their uniforms in perfect condition, it was all about making the dreaded drill instructor look good when his unit was inspected by a higher-ranking officer.

When a military unit marches, there is a special banner that is carried by the first person on the first row. It designates that unit's distinctive job, the rank of the men, etc. This flag is called the "guide on." I will never forget when we attended our son's graduation from a military school. He was allowed to come off base with us the night before his graduation. He entertained us all evening with stories of how, during their three-month-long special schooling, his unit had repeatedly "lost the guide on." This meant that due to some minor infraction of the rules, their special banner had been given to another unit's commander. And then they would have to prove themselves worthy to get it back. Kyer had us laughing until we cried as he regaled us with stories about one young man in his unit who had a bit of a speech impediment, and would plead in a high-pitched sort of whine, "Guys, we got to get the guide on back!" By this time in his career as a soldier, Kyer had come to understand that it was all sort of a big "war game," and that before the unit would graduate, the commander would always find some way to deliver their guide on back to them. There was, in other words, really nothing to worry about.

Yet this one young man, whose family was coming for the graduation, fretted repeatedly about how they would have to march without their guide on. He did not want to be embarrassed, nor did he want his commanding officer to have the humiliation of marching a unit whose guide on was being carried by another unit. If that young man had been a bird, I believe he might have been a cardinal, holding his head high because he knew he was making his commander look good by keeping the guide on where it should be.

Many years later, I applied for a job as the administrative assistant to the president of a large corporation which is run on Christian principles. I was not qualified for that job in any way, shape or form. But I thought it would not hurt to apply. Imagine my surprise when I was hired! After some time had passed and I had grown more comfortable in the position, I asked the vice president of the company why I had been hired. He said, "Not for your skills, that is for sure!" with a laugh. Then he said, "Skills can be taught,

Raelene. Attitude can't." Apparently on the day of my initial interview, I had unknowingly displayed some godly qualities that impressed the man who would be my boss. He wanted someone in that position who he felt would make him look good by having the right kind of attitude when the matters of business became pressing. Knowing this made me try very hard to always do my best and even to look my best. I wanted to be like the cardinals. We need to pray that we would be like the cardinals of nature, always making our God look good.

We had a man in one of the churches we pastored who was a cardinal. He served in nearly every position there is within our local church body. At one time or other he had been Sunday School Superintendent, head usher, greeter, treasurer, board member, teacher, and just about anything else you can name. He was almost always the first person through the doors on Sunday mornings, and I was so thankful for that. It began my pastor-husband's day on such a positive note to be able to spend a few minutes laughing with this man before the rest of the crowd came in. He sat through countless board meetings, congregational meetings and Sunday School staff meetings. Anyone who has served in any capacity in a church knows that there are times when these meetings can explode into rather heated discussions. People have their own opinion as to how things should be done, and some can get very vocal and upset if others don't agree with their opinions. But my husband tells me that in the years that we served at this church, he never saw this dear cardinal of a man become upset over anything. He just quietly did his many jobs and made God look good to those he came in contact with, whether they were inside or outside the family of God.

This man was also very conscious of the needs and de-
sires of his wife. We have been out to eat with them several
times, and one can almost envision the two of them feeding
each other seeds of love as the cardinals do. Evidently they
take the teachings of our Lord seriously when He instructed
us to "Let your light so shine before men that they may see
your good works and glorify your Father which is in
heaven." This man's light shines—if he were a bird, he
would definitely be a bright red cardinal. And his slightly
less colorful, orange-feathered wife would be by his side,
ever working to make her husband and her Creator look
good.

## Showing the Creator to Others

Our denomination operates a "family camp" in late July
and early August each summer. This is unique among
church camping experiences in many ways. The entire
family attends the camp together. However, there is a full
youth camp which is operating at the same time. So, middle
and high school age youth are off "doing their own thing"
during much of the day. And they stay in chaperoned cabins
with their peers at night, rather than in the family cabins,
tents, or campers. But everyone comes together for one
large evening service in an open-air tabernacle. We also eat
our meals with the teens. It is not uncommon for the camp
to have 500 or more people in attendance, and over 100 of
those will be youth campers.

Many years ago, the evangelist who spoke in all the services at one camp was a small, rather nerdy-looking
Canadian man. When our kids, who were teenagers at the
time, first saw him, they were not excited. He had white
hair and looked very conservative. I think the kids immedi-

ately judged him to be too old-fashioned to relate to their 1980s-style needs. He had a rich Canadian accent and he did a lot of shouting as he preached. It was very interesting to watch the attitudes of the teens change as the week progressed. Reverend Ethan Parker was a cardinal! He made God look very good to the rowdy group of teens on the campground that week. He loved each teen unconditionally and preached Jesus to them, not only by his words but by his actions. He chose to eat his meals with the kids, oftentimes waiting in a long line while the other adults on the grounds were served first. He talked with them and had the joy of praying with many of them.

Weather-wise, it was a horrible week. I think it rained every day. During times when the teens would normally have been on the ball fields or the volleyball courts, they were stuck in their cabins watching thunderstorm after thunderstorm. After several days of this, the dirt infield on the ball diamond had turned into a quagmire. In desperation, the director of teen camp decided to let the kids have some mud games. We adults watched in horror as they slid their way through races and relays, eventually falling and being covered in dark brown mud from head to toe. Those who did not fall into the mud, dove in headfirst and came up with only their eyes shining through the mess. When another thunderstorm hit, the games were over. We were back in our cabin when we heard a large contingency of the teenage boys racing through the camp shouting, "Rev. Parker! Come out, come out, wherever you are!" Eventually the little evangelist popped his head out the door of his camper where he had evidently been taking a brief nap. The kids grabbed him and pulled him out of the camper. One by one these mud-covered guys gave him a big bear hug. The last one in the line even ran his muddy fingers through the white hair which had always been impeccably combed, until now. The little evangelist laughed and laughed, all the way to the showers.

During that week of camp, Rev. Parker taught the entire group of us a Scripture chorus. He was not a great singer, and there didn't seem to be any printed versions of this music. He croaked it to us line by line and we followed his lead, singing a cappella. It was simply the words of I Peter 2:9, "But you are a chosen people, a royal priesthood, a holy nation, a people belonging to God, that you may declare the praises of him who called you out of darkness into his wonderful light."

When the last night of camp came, the teens were sad to leave behind the man who had shown them the love of Jesus in such a marvelous way. As we sang the chorus, there were tears in their eyes because here was a man who had shown them by his actions what it was like to be part of a chosen people, a royal priesthood. Some of them had gotten permission from the camp staff to show their love to Rev. Parker in a special way. As we began to sing, a huge Canadian flag unfurled itself from the rafters at the back of the tabernacle. The kids applauded. Rev. Parker was dumbstruck! He just kept singing the chorus, as tears flowed down his cheeks.

If we had all been birds that week, Rev. Ethan Parker would definitely have been a cardinal. For, in the words of the Scripture chorus, does not a cardinal know how to "declare the praises of him who called you out of darkness into his wonderful light"?

When I see a bright flash of red feathers against the snow this winter, I pray that God will remind me of the words of the old catechism regarding the chief aim of man.

We are here so that we may, like the cardinal, glorify God! I want to make my Creator look good.

## Chapter Seven

# *Turkey Vultures*

Can there be an uglier creature alive than the common turkey vulture? Until we moved to the country, I had never seen one of these birds up close and personal. I had often seen them circling in the sky and remembered that my dad always declared, "There is something dead somewhere." Looking at them from a distance, they appear to be big black birds whose wings slant upward as they make huge circles in the sky. When we lived in the country on Cowpath Road, I met these birds on a regular basis as they feasted on roadkill. They are some of the most repulsive creatures I have ever seen.

The turkey vulture has a short, squatty body with wings

that stick out over its tail. In a mature bird, the wings are often more than three times the length of the body. Its feathers are black and brown. If you drive by one of these predators while they are eating, you will find that their feathers are often filthy, caked with the dried blood and rotting flesh of the dead animal they are consuming. More noticeable than the dirt on its body, however, is the bird's ugly red head. He has no feathers at all on his head, which appears to be bright red, wrinkled flesh. His eyes are set low on his face and are ringed in yellow. His head protrudes forward into a sharp beak that appears to have a definite overbite. I doubt there is anyone alive, except for another turkey vulture, that would call it a beautiful bird.

One of the reasons we humans find the birds to be so detestable is because they eat the rotting bodies of dead animals. In fact, a turkey vulture would starve if not for the death of other animals. Scientists tell us that his claws are dull on his chicken-shaped feet, which is compounded by the fact that his ugly beak is very thin and weak. The bird is incapable of killing anything itself, so it feasts on the spoils of other hunting animals, animals that meet their death by natural causes or (probably most frequently) animals that have been hit by cars. However, due to the weaknesses inherent in a turkey vulture's talons and beak, it must often wait for another animal to initially tear into a fresh kill. Its only other option is to wait for the dead body to begin to decay so that it will be easier for the bird to break into the flesh.

## A Job to Do

What can we learn from this ugly animal with its disgusting eating habits? Why should a chapter of this book be devoted to this nasty bird? A biblical truth that needs to be applied in all areas of life is clearly demonstrated by the very presence of turkey vultures in our world. Every creation of God (no matter how it may seem to humankind) is placed on this earth with a job to do. The turkey vulture performs his task exactly as the Creator intends, without ever getting any thanks or appreciation from the rest of the world.

Scientists tell us that without the turkey vultures, disease would run rampant among farm animals and wild animals alike. The turkey vulture's digestive tract has the amazing ability to kill bacteria, whether from the maggot-infested carcass of a raccoon killed by a speeding car or from a cow that dies of mad cow disease or anthrax. Somehow the product of the turkey vulture's own excrement is re-ingested and takes care of all the diseases that would normally enter his mouth through his horrible diet. So, even though much of what a turkey vulture eats is disease-laden, the bird itself remains healthy. In this way, the turkey vulture rids the earth of lots of bacteria and disease. Scientists are certain that these birds and their eating habits have saved the world from countless epidemics.

Since a turkey vulture never bathes in water, after his meal has been completed, he can often be seen cleaning his feathers and wings by scraping the entire length of each feather with his beak. It appears that his dessert after a meal is the garbage that has gotten all over his body! The one area the bird is incapable of cleaning is the ugly red top of its head. Perhaps that is the reason you can see the turkey vulture standing with his wings spread in bright sunlight. I wonder if he knows that the radiation present in the sun's rays will help to clean his body (mainly the top of his head) of bacteria? Or does it simply feel good to him to stand in the hot noonday sun?

If birds talk to each other, the turkey vulture does not join the conversation. The only noise he is capable of making is a hissing, which is produced by blowing through his huge, prominent nostrils. So while the smaller songbirds and others converse, the ugly turkey vulture remains mute. He has probably never had any other creature thank him for his contribution to life as we know it on planet earth. He is, perhaps, the most unappreciated of all birds.

## Appreciation Is Due

Many of God's servants feel unappreciated. How many church janitors ever receive a "thank you" for a job well done? People are sure to notice if the Communion table has dust on it and complain. But does anyone ever thank the person who normally keeps it and the rest of the sanctuary spotless? Ushers are another unappreciated group of God's servants. These are men who steadfastly stand at the door of the church week in and week out to greet people and usher them to their pews. I wonder how many of them are thanked for their faithfulness? And then there are the people who care for other people's children in the church nursery. As they wipe snotty little noses and try to comfort the toddlers who want their mommy, do they ever feel un-appreciated?

In recent years, radio and TV ministries, in conjunction with manufacturers of Christian greeting cards, have begun to emphasize that October is "Pastor Appreciation Month." When this tradition began, it was suggested that one partic-ular Sunday should be designated as a time to say thank you to the pastor for all he has done. As the phenomenon grew, it expanded to an entire month being set aside for people to acknowledge their pastor's untiring ministry. As a pastor's wife, of course, I am very thankful for this show of support. Our churches have done wonderful things for us, from sending us away for a little "R and R" at a lovely state park lodge to giving us gifts. The first year that we served in a rural church, each family was encouraged to be creative and give us a gift of time spent with them in different ways. One of our Pastor Appreciation gifts that year was the opportunity to ride on a combine and view the harvesting of crops. My husband sneezed for several days afterward, but we were being loved and accepted in spite of our citified ways. What bothers Dan and I, though, are the many choice servants of God who never get recognized or thanked for the work that they do by anyone here on earth. Like the turkey vultures and their relationship to the earth's ecosystem, some people quietly perform various services for the family of God, and no one ever says thank you.

One such group of ministers is those who work all across our nation in inner-city Rescue Missions. Early in our ministry, we had the opportunity to live and work at the Children's Chapel of the Lima Rescue Home in Lima, Ohio. When we first told people that we felt God was calling us to go there, we were unprepared for the negative responses we would receive. We were excited by the opportunities we would have to share Jesus with children who lived "on the wrong side of the tracks," so to speak. But good, well-meaning Christian people told us that we were crazy to even think of moving our young family into that horrible neighborhood to try to help the children who lived in the area. Their reactions were so hard for us to understand. We had expected that our worldly friends and acquaintances would think we had lost our minds. But when some of our family and other friends got so upset over our choice, we had to go to our knees. Thankfully, we received confirmation from our heavenly Father: "If you have done it unto one of the least of these, my brethren, you have done it unto me."

We lived at the Chapel for two years. The age span of the children we worked with ranged from preschool to high school. One evening when we came home from a rather late night church activity, we found a little three-year-old girl sitting on our front porch. Recognizing her from Bible class, we took her into our upstairs apartment and asked why she was out so late at night. With her limited verbal skills, she explained, "I cain't go home till that big car be gone from my house." Evidently, her mother had a gentleman caller who did not like children. So, the child had been placed outside at 10 P.M. in this extremely rough neighborhood and told not to return until the Cadillac was gone. We rocked her and checked the street periodically. My husband carried her home when the car was gone in the wee hours of the morning. No one thanked us for taking care of this child.

One of our biggest challenges in the Rescue Mission work was a boy named Ruben who was about five feet tall and weighed about 300 pounds. He was the oldest child in a clan of brothers, sisters, cousins, nieces and nephews. There were about 20 of them who were all related to Ruben in various ways. Ruben invented the word ornery. He was always pulling practical jokes and keeping us laughing. But, he also had a mean side to him, and then the orneriness was not so funny.

One day that will always stand out in our minds was the day when Ruben organized a mutiny at Camp Roberts. This wonderful day camp is in the country, about 15 miles from

Lima. Our summers consisted of taking van loads of children out of the city, away from the dirt and grime where they were growing up, to a wonderful plot of ground that had been developed into a camp by the owners of the Rescue Mission. For many of these kids, their week at camp was the first time they had ever been outside the city limits. They were both excited and a little frightened to go on this adventure. We sang songs about Jesus in the vans and hit the ground running when we arrived. The days consisted of swimming in a spotlessly clean pool, playing big games of softball, kickball or other sports, and then a time of Bible stories and learning, all in the fresh country air. We fed them nutritious food and tried to show them the love of Christ. They were tiring days, but we felt we were making some headway toward introducing them to the Savior.

Then came the day that Ruben Miller got upset over some minor disagreement with one of the counselors and tried to get the counselor to fight. When the young man refused to get into fisticuffs with the teenager, Ruben blew up! He cussed him up one side and down the other and exclaimed, "I ain't gonna stay at your stupid old camp! C'mon, Millers! We're outta here." About 15 of our older campers, all bigger and stronger than many of the staff, decided they were going to walk home. Of course we could not allow that! They trudged through the forest to the gate and were almost to a busy highway before we decided that perhaps the best thing we could do was simply to grant them their request and take them home for the day! So we loaded them into the vans and brought them back into town, with Ruben screaming every inch of the way that he did not have to obey our stupid honky rules, and he was never going to come to our Bible classes again.

We certainly felt defeated and unappreciated that night, and indeed for the rest of that summer as the Miller clan continued to refuse to participate in any Rescue Mission activity.

Many years later, when the days we served at the Mission were a distant memory, our daughter was home from college for Christmas, and we were visiting family in the Lima area. One afternoon, Sonya and I decided to go to the mall for some last-minute shopping. As we walked through the mall, suddenly I was grabbed from behind and lifted off the ground in a big bear hug. I looked down to see two very black, very strong arms encircling me. I remember thinking, "I am going to die. Right here in the Lima Mall, I am going to be killed." Sonya screamed and jumped away from the tussle that ensued as my assailant spun me around to look him in the face. "Raelene, don't you recognize me?" asked the handsome, young African American male. I looked into his eyes and saw the same ornery gleam that had been there all those years before at the Mission Children's Chapel.

"Ruben? Ruben Miller?" I gasped. By this time, Sonya realized we had nothing to fear, and she began to laugh. "Aren't you the kid who got upset and left camp?"

Tears were streaming down Ruben's face by this time. Imagine our surprise as he told us that he wished he could go back and relive his middle and high school days. He said that when he quit going to Bible class, he became deeply involved in the drug scene that is so rampant in the city. He proceeded to tell us about each member of his clan, and what prison they were in for what crime.

"I was in prison, too. In fact, I had no hope of parole. I had been sent away so many times on so many different charges. But, Raelene, do you know what happened? One night I awoke from a sound sleep there in my cell. I had been dreaming. In the dream, I was back at Camp Roberts, and we were singing a song about Jesus."

He stopped at this point of the narrative and began to sing the song for us. My very shy daughter glanced around at the other shoppers, who were visibly startled by this scene—a black man crying as he talked to two white women and then burst into song. However, Ruben's sincerity soon dispatched our fears of what others were thinking. He proceeded with his story.

"That night in the prison, I fell on my knees at the edge of my cot and prayed, 'Jesus, if You really are there and if You really are God, please come into my heart like they said You would. Take away my sin and let me live my life for You.'"

By now there were tears on both my face and my daughter's. Ruben picked me up again in another bear hug. "Raelene, Jesus did come in my heart that night. He changed my life! I got out of prison, and now my whole reason for living is to tell people that He loves them and will help them, too." As he put me down for the second time, he asked about my husband.

"When you get home," he pleaded, "will you tell Dan that one of the kids he worked so hard with all those years ago has come to know Jesus? Will you tell him that I thank him and you for living there at the Chapel and for giving your lives so that bratty little kids like me would come to know our wonderful Lord? Promise me that you will tell him how thankful I am." I promised.

At that time, singer Ray Boltz had just recorded a song called "Thank You." The lyrics are about a Sunday School teacher who never knows until he gets to heaven that one of the children in his class has been saved. It also tells about the work of missionaries that is "unnoticed on the earth" but gets acclaim in heaven. As we walked away from Ruben that evening, Sonya said, "Mom, the song 'Thank You' just happened to you—right in the middle of the Lima Mall!" She was right.

Ruben ran a shoeshine stand in downtown Lima, very close to the area where we had lived when we first met him. He also sold Christian t-shirts and was somewhat of a "street preacher." He witnessed to everyone who would listen about how he got saved while he was in prison, all because of lessons and songs he had heard as a child at Bible classes and at camp.

A few years ago, Ruben died. He had abused his body so badly with drugs and alcohol during his formative years that eventually it had caught up with him. But, I am positive that we will see Ruben Miller again. For Jesus had come into his life. He will be waiting for us in heaven.

And so, now as I travel the lonely country road around where we live and see the ugly turkey vultures as they make a meal of the opossum or raccoon that just wasn't quite fast enough to make it across the road, I think about the day God allowed me to get a little thanks for an otherwise unrewarding job. Since I have learned of the debt we owe to this bird, for ridding our area of diseased animals, I try not to turn away in disgust. I look at the bird's ugly red head and whisper, "Thank you."

Chapter Eight

*Turkeys*

erhaps one of the most classic art projects children in kindergartens across our fair land do every fall is to trace around their chubby little hand, add a face to the tracing of their thumb, and color the tracings of their four fingers in brilliant hues. Voila! A beautiful turkey is born for Mom to hang on the front of the refrigerator and display proudly. Of course, this project is completed some time early in the month of November. Teachers everywhere try to instill in children the wonders of the magnificent birds who were featured at that first Thanksgiving feast back in 1621. The pictures in the storybooks show the Indians and Pilgrims sitting down to eat together, and there is always a huge golden brown bird prominently displayed on the table. It is enough to get the taste buds working overtime just to see the picture. I don't know if turkey was really served at that first feast of gratitude or not, but I do know that in the vast majority of homes today, there is a bird on the table on the fourth Thursday of November every year.

From our earliest days, we are taught to connect giving thanks to the largest game bird that graces our shores—the magnificent eastern turkey. What child has not proclaimed to everyone at the Thanksgiving celebration that they will eat an entire drumstick, only to find that their little tummies are too full after only half the turkey leg has been consumed? And who has not vied for the honor of pulling the wishbone, perhaps truly believing (at least at an early age) that the person who gets the larger side of the broken bone will have their wish come true? No other bird can claim such universal recognition, though very few people have the privilege of seeing the big bird in the wild. Indeed, many a small child probably thinks of the bird only as a part of a delicious feast, not as a wonderful creation of God from which we can learn valuable lessons.

"Turkeys have waddles and caruncles," the science teacher said. I remember thinking that waddling was something that overweight people did when they walked. And, what on earth were caruncles, unless of course it was the husband of a car-aunt or the parent of a car-niece or car-nephew?

I soon learned that the turkey's waddle is what I had always referred to as the "red, hangie-down thing" under the turkey's neck. I thought it was the way to tell a boy turkey from a girl turkey, but I learned that even the female bird begins to have a waddle after she reaches maturity, though hers is never quite as noticeable as that of her male counterpart.

The caruncles are areas of smooth, feather-free skin on the bird's head, and the side and back of the neck. The frontal caruncle is a wart-like growth that grows at the base of the turkey's beak, where the beak attaches to the face. On the female bird it looks like a little bump, giving the bird the appearance of having a nose. On the male, it appears that this little bump has grown like the proboscis of an alcoholic man—it is large and very red. Sometimes it is so large that it hangs down several inches off the bird's face. But the turkey has the ability to also make it contract, so when viewed at a different time, the frontal caruncle can look like a tight little horn sticking straight up in the air.

Turkeys are one of the most colorful birds I have studied. Their feathers often appear to change colors. Scientists say that the reason for this has something to do with the ability of their feathers to reflect light differently than those of other birds. I suppose this is true since the turkey has different types of feathers, and each seems to have its own particular function. Down feathers lie flat against the body surface and provide warmth, while vein feathers provide an outer layer to the bird. These vein feathers reflect light because of tiny, transparent platelets that cover their surface. As the bird turns in the sun, you can see him change from brown to green to shades of blue and sometimes even red—all due to the way the light is reflected on the platelets. God has given the bird the amazing instinct to protect itself in cold winter weather by using its feathers to the best of their insulating abilities. Turkeys are often seen wandering about in wintry weather, but they are always smart enough to face themselves into a strong cold wind. Turning into the wind keeps their vein feathers from being ruffled and allows the down feathers to hold the heat against their body. Perhaps we humans could learn that we are better off when we do not allow our "feathers to be ruffled" by the winds of adversity we sometimes face.

The more amazing ability of the great turkey regarding color is seen in the bird's face, waddles, and caruncles. A quick glance at a turkey can tell many things about how the bird is feeling. He might be called "the bird that cannot hide his true feelings." For, you see, if the bird is frightened, his face and the accompanying extra skin of the waddle and caruncles will become a pale bluish-white. More of us have seen the turkey when this is his coloring rather than any other way. The reason is obvious. If we are seeing him, he is likely seeing us also and is therefore frightened.

During mating season, the waddle and caruncles are bright red. Scientists say that the happy bird's blood pressure increases as he struts to attract his mate. He fans his wonderful tail feathers, drops his pale face back against the waddle, expands the frontal caruncle and proudly walks back and forth in front of his girlfriend as if to say, "Look at my glorious colors. You know you want me!"

The changing colors of the turkey remind me of the "mood ring" craze of the late 1960s and early 1970s. A ring with a black stone was placed on the finger. Supposedly if the person wearing the ring's mood changed, so did the color of the stone. I imagine that there was a scientific reason the stone would change—sweaty palms or maybe the soap used in washing one's hands. With the turkey, however, the color change is all built into his system by our wonderful Creator, not by some shyster who is trying to sell cheap jewelry. The turkey cannot hide his feelings.

## Being Transparent

I wonder, wouldn't the church be better off if people did not try to hide their feelings? On the average Sunday morning in the average church in America, a typical greeting from one congregant to another is, "Good morning. How are you?" But, do we really want an answer to that question?

How would we respond if the person we had just greeted were to answer, "Well, I am not doing very well. You see, my husband screamed at the kids on the way to church. And my parents are both aging very dramatically, and there is nothing I can do to stop it. It looks like I might lose my job this week, and the washing machine broke down yesterday. How am I? Well, actually, I feel really rotten—but thank you for your concern." If people responded to us like that, we'd have the opportunity to stand with them in prayer, show compassion, and perhaps find a way to meet one of their needs.

But instead of being transparent like the turkey, we paste on our happy go-to-church smiles, and lie by saying everything is fine. Perhaps the church has not really learned the truths taught by Paul in II Corinthians 1: "God comforts us in all our tribulation, that we may be able to comfort those who are in any trouble with the comfort with which we ourselves are comforted by God" (verses 3-4). When people are hurting, those of us in the family of God need to comfort them—not make them feel as if they should not share their problems. If, like the turkey, our faces truly reflected how we felt, perhaps we would all be healthier Christians.

When my husband had chosen to leave pastoral ministry for awhile, we moved with the military to our state's capital.

We had just come through some rather tough struggles in a church family, so we were leery about getting involved in church again. And yet, we soon found that staying home and avoiding the family of God was not the answer. So we began to search for a church family. We tried many different churches, but kept coming away with the same feeling. Discouraged, we would say to each other, "The pastor just doesn't seem real." Perhaps we were too judgmental. If we had given the men more than just a few weeks' trial period, maybe we would have found a pastor we could trust. But repeatedly we ran into men who seemed to be trying to make a name for themselves, rather than ones who would preach, "Thus saith the Lord."

One common characteristic of these men was that they did not look at you as they were talking to you. Now I don't mean when they were in the pulpit—for there are always differing amounts of eye contact at that point. I am talking about when we were in a one-on-one situation. Often it seemed that they were looking over our heads (which is hard to do with my 6 foot 3 inch husband!) to see if there was someone else they needed to speak with. We would wonder: Was it someone who could give more to the church's building fund? Was it someone who had a more important position in the Body? Was it a prospective member? Why was it that the preacher could not fully concentrate on speaking with us? Why did he have to wonder whom he was missing while listening to us?

Then we went to a different church, where we met Rev. Melvin Schmidt. He is a rather short man who is balding and not overly attractive, until you get to know his heart. And, like the turkey, it did not take long for us to determine his feelings. Oh, he did not change colors. But he definitely did not try to hide how he felt. Most of the time he was like a cheerleader—extremely positive, outgoing, fun, and almost bouncy! But there were times when his countenance would be very different—sad, dark, and some might say moody. It was easy to tell when he was burdened; he did not try to hide it. In fact, some in the congregation probably wished he were not quite so transparent. But, to Dan and I, Pastor Mel was like a breath of fresh air after our many encounters with fake people.

We had been attending this church for about a month and were driving the few blocks home when I turned to Dan and asked, "Do you think there is any chance that Pastor Mel is for real? Do you think anyone cares as much about people as he seems to?" I remember that my husband's response was, "Well, if he doesn't truly care, he is doing the best job of faking it of anyone I have ever seen."

We would soon find out that Rev. Schmidt was indeed "the real deal." Dan and I went through some deep waters while we lived in Delaware. He was sent away for several Army schoolings, and it was during one of those times that my world came crashing down. Unbeknownst to us, our two adult children had both been going through trouble of their own. Within just a few months of each other, our kids were each facing divorce. I wondered if I would ever be able to quit crying. I could see no light at the end of the tunnel. I blamed myself for their problems, even though they lived many states away from us. I knew in my heart that God had promised never to allow more than I could bear, but every night I cried out that this was getting pretty close.

It was then that Pastor Mel and his dear wife, Elsie, proved over and over that the caring we had observed and wondered about was indeed real. If Mel had been born a turkey, I am not sure what color his waddle and caruncle would have been—but I know that I did not have to wonder what he was feeling. He cried with us. He pointed us to the Psalms and told us God was big enough to handle our frustrations, just like He had King David's. He encouraged us not to try to hide the way we were feeling. He said, "The church can only be the church when its members do not try to disguise the hurt they are going through."

And so, with the help of our dear little pastor, we survived that awful time in our lives. In fact, as bad as it was, we have since been able to do as we are instructed in that first chapter of II Corinthians and "comfort others with the comfort with which we ourselves had been comforted by God." I often wonder if we would have ever been willing to even consider coming back into full-time pastoral ministry ourselves if we had not met Pastor Melvin Schmidt. We are eternally grateful—and when we say he is a real "turkey" of a man, it is a compliment!

## God Used a Turkey

A chapter about turkeys would not be complete in my book without the amazing story of my son-in-law's conversion. Because, you see, a turkey was used by God to lead our daughter's new husband to Jesus!

Jamie has been an outdoorsman extraordinaire for his entire adult life. My husband Dan likes spectator sports and enjoys playing softball and basketball. Jamie, however, has introduced our family to the fascinating world of hunting and fishing—and not just for the small lake fish and squirrels. Jamie has taken Sonya deep-sea fishing. They have pictures of Sonya standing on a pier with her arm around the shark she caught, and the shark is several feet taller than our daughter. Jamie has also taken Sonya to firing ranges, where she has proved herself to be quite a markswoman. Jamie has hunted for bear in northern Canada, as well as the more traditional deer here in the States. He hunts with bow and/or gun—whichever is in season. Their freezer is usually full of venison. But Jamie's favorite thing to hunt is the majestic bird that Benjamin Franklin nominated to be the national symbol of America—the eastern turkey.

When Jamie and Sonya had been dating for awhile, their friendship was growing deeper, and they had begun to talk about spiritual things. They were reading the *Left Behind* series of books by Jenkins and LaHaye. Jamie had begun to think about his need for a relationship with God through Jesus.

One morning, Jamie got up before dawn and headed into a remote area of woods in the mountains of North Carolina to hunt for turkeys. He had done the same thing countless other times, and even had the mounted tail feathers of his largest kill to prove it. This time, though, something was different. As he walked through the woods in that pre-dawn stillness, he began to hear something. Jaime said it felt as though something was hunting him! In that remote area, it could have been a bear or a wildcat. He began to sweat. He said that he would walk a few steps, hearing something behind him. When he stopped, the movement behind him also stopped. For the first time in his life, he felt as though he might die. He was beginning to be "scared to death." And he knew that if this nameless something were to actually attack and kill him, he was not ready to die because he had never made his peace with God.

So, right there, in the middle of his quest for a turkey, Jamie knelt by an old log in the woods and began to pray.

He relates that he confessed all his sins, and asked Jesus to come into his life. God met him in the woods that day. There was rejoicing in the presence of the angels as the young man, who was to later become a member of our family, repented and became a Christian.

Imagine Sonya's surprise when he came to her house later in the day to relate that he had not caught a turkey! She knew from past experiences that a fruitless hunt would normally make for a depressed Jamie. Yet, there he was, smiling from ear to ear. He had found something of eternal consequence on his hunt that day—a lasting relationship with the One who had created the turkey in the first place. Since that time, it has been our joy to watch Jamie grow spiritually. He and Sonya were united in marriage later that year. He promises that some fine day he will fix us a turkey to eat that he has personally killed, dressed out, and prepared in the southern way—frying it in a deep fat fryer.

From my first knowledge of the turkey, when I traced my hand in kindergarten, until we heard Jamie's story, there is only one word that I associate with this magnificent bird—thanksgiving!

## Chapter Nine

# *Robins*

In the Midwest we have four very distinct seasons. When Dan was in the military in the early days of our marriage, we lived in California where the seasons did not change. We did not get to see leaves change colors or stand at a window and watch snow fall. It seemed to us that life took on a horrible sameness, and we truly missed the seasonal changes in the weather and the land-scape. Now that we are growing older, it is hard to imagine that we truly missed the sometimes bitter cold of an Ohio winter. And yet, even now, if we were to move to a milder climate, I know that I would miss the ever-changing panorama of weather we enjoy (or not enjoy, as the case may be) here in the Midwest.

Perhaps only one who has endured a dreadful, bitter cold winter can truly experience the hope that is felt by Midwesterners when they first view a robin in springtime! The robin is the first migrating bird to return to our area each year. In some elementary school classrooms, teachers hold a yearly contest with a prize given to the first child who spots the bird with the red breast. We are taught the word "harbinger" at a young age, when we learn that Mr. Robin is the first harbinger of spring. He is indeed "one who goes before, heralding something that is coming soon."

## The Message of Hope

A few years ago I experienced one of the longest winters of my life. In mid-November I had surgery on my foot to correct a bunion and some hammertoe problems. I purposely planned to have this done in the winter, because I knew that I would not even want to be doing much outside at that time of the year. So I thought, *If I have to convalesce with my foot raised in the air, it might as well be at a time when being rather dormant is forced upon us Midwesterners anyway.* I was in a hard cast for a couple of weeks. When that came off, I was placed in a removable "boot." Though the boot is designed in such a way that one can walk on it, my doctor instructed me not to put any pressure on my foot at all for 11 long weeks. Up until that time, I had no idea how hard it is to get around on crutches and not place any weight at all on one's foot. I sat in a recliner and watched TV or read until I thought I would go completely bonkers. Periodically I maneuvered the crutches into just the right place and took a "stroll" down the hallway of our home or maybe to the kitchen to look out a different window. But within just a few minutes I would be hobbling back to my chair, exhausted from the effort.

Christmas that year was not a real fun time for me. I sat in the chair and watched Dan decorate the house. I did not do any baking, except what I had done before the surgery and put into our freezer. I was able to help wrap some presents, but even that was not an easy task. It seemed the tape was always at the other end of the table. Some folks in the church invited us to come to their home and have Christmas dinner with them. They live in a split-level home with very steep stairs leading up to their dining room. After trying valiantly to maneuver the stairs with crutches, I gave up and sat down on the steps. Dragging myself up the steps backwards was more than a little humiliating. I vowed that if I ever made it back down those stairs, I would gladly go back home to the parsonage and stay put until the foot had healed.

It was a hard winter weather-wise too, so the view from every window was the same—a world of white seemed to have enveloped us. The snow came daily for a couple weeks and by the time we got our first break, there were drifts nearly five feet deep in our yard. I didn't even try to make it across the parking lot to our church services. Basically, I was totally shut in for that entire 11 weeks.

At last came the day when the doctor had promised the boot would be removed and I would graduate down to a sort of "shoe" that was really just a sole with some cloth sides and Velcro straps to keep it tight against the healing foot. There was still a lot of snow on the ground, so walking up the icy sidewalk into the doctor's office seemed rather perilous. Dan stopped the car at the end of the walk and went into the office to get a wheelchair for me. (Since this doctor specializes in foot surgery, there are always two or three wheelchairs immediately inside his office door.) He wheeled me into the reception area, and my favorite nurse greeted me with, "Today's the day, huh, Raelene?"

The doctor took x-rays yet again, to make sure that the bones he had fused were knitting together properly. Imagine my dismay when the nurse entered my examining room with the dreaded boot in her hand and a sad look on her face. "Two more weeks." She explained, "We want to make sure the bones are completely healed before we allow you to put any pressure on your foot."

I had thought I would walk out of the office. Dan wheeled me to the car, again borrowing the wheelchair. As he returned the chair to the office, the waterworks started for me! I wasn't sure I could endure two more weeks of this forced rest. Our car was parked at the edge of the doctor's parking lot that is lined with some lovely shrubbery. I am not sure what the name of the plant is, but the leaves remain a waxy green throughout the winter. I was wiping my eyes and having a little private pity party when Dan returned and told me to look under the bushes. There, hopping all over the ground below the hedge, were five gorgeous robins! They were fat and happy, so I presumed they had made the northward migration very recently since there were several inches of snow and ice keeping them from finding worms here. Discouraged as I was, I felt my tear-stained face breaking into a big grin. Mixing a couple of famous quotes I said, "If robins come, can spring be far behind?" Seeing those beautiful birds gave me hope. Two weeks later, when the foot was declared to be healed enough for me to walk on it, the ground was also free of snow. We parked in the same place and saw that the robins were working on building a nest at the base of the shrubs. I was reminded that God promised Noah in Genesis 8:22 there will always be both seedtime and harvest. In our area of the country, seedtime, or spring, is always heralded by robins. No wonder they are often referred to as the bird of hope!

Robins seem to evoke happy thoughts in all who see them. Perhaps more songs have been written about robins than any other bird. And there are nursery rhymes and children's stories in abundance about the red-breasted bird. Whether one thinks of the song which tells of the "red, red robin" who "comes bob, bob, bobbing along" or the tale of Mr. Robin Redbreast read as a bedtime story, the message of this bird always seems to be happy and hopeful.

## Bringing Hope to Youngsters

Because of the writing I have done, I often get the opportunity to speak. One of my favorite places to speak is in a public middle school setting. It is an invigorating challenge to try to bring a bit of hope into the lives of today's average 12 to 14-year-old students. Upon my arrival, I often ask the kids what their goals are for the future. Gone are the days when kids respond with "I want to be a fireman" or "I want to be a secretary." It seems that they either have totally unrealistic goals like "I am going to play tight end for the Dallas Cowboys," or they have no goals at all! It is this latter group that concerns me. They feel there is no reason to hope for anything because the future is so uncertain. This attitude was especially evident shortly after the tragedy that befell America on September 11, 2001. When I spoke to a group of students that fall, they all expressed the same thing. They doubted they would live to be adults, so they saw no reason to make any plans or prepare for a future they were unlikely to ever realize.

As I have for years, I pointed those kids in 2001 to some

classic literature of days long gone. Some of the girls, with their heavy eye make-up and bleached hair, feel they are too sophisticated to bother with it. But I have found that if they can be challenged to try reading some stories that have been loved down through the ages, they begin to realize that although we live in an uncertain world, hope does indeed spring eternal. Whether they read Eleanor Porter's *Pollyanna*, Johanna Spyri's *Heidi*, or my personal favorite, L.M. Montgomery's *Anne of Green Gables*, they find a heroine that continues to hope—no matter what.

Pollyanna is hoping for the day when her Aunt Polly will love her. Heidi hopes for so many things in her story, but perhaps none is more poignant than her desire to see her grandfather rekindle his seemingly lost relationship with God. In the beloved series of *Anne of Green Gables* books, little Anne Shirley first hopes that she will be adopted. Then she hopes to best Gilbert Blythe in the daily competitions for grades in the one-room school. She hopes that she and Diana will always be friends. Her life story is all about hoping—but, in reality, isn't that true for every person ever born? When the middle school students begin to analyze these old classic stories, they find that every generation has had reasons to be hopeless, but with only a small amount of effort, hope can be reborn. All we need to do is look at a robin in springtime to realize this truth.

One of my favorite portions of the Bible is the little book of Ruth. Only four chapters long, it is tucked away in the Old Testament and often overlooked. At the beginning of the book, a woman named Naomi traveled with her husband, Elimelech, from Bethlehem to Moab. There was a famine in the land around their home, so they felt that moving into Moab would help them save themselves and their two sons from certain death. However, Elimelech died in the new land, leaving Naomi as a widow with her two sons. Perhaps the devastated Naomi began to hope for a future again as her sons each found a wife—Orpah and Ruth. Naomi probably thought, *I may not be a wife, but surely I will be a grandmother soon.* However, her hopes were crushed again about 10 years later when both of her sons died before any children had been born to either of them.

Naomi found herself completely bereft, a hopeless old lady living in a foreign land, with no true relatives or loved ones nearby except her two daughters-in-law. Not wanting to be a burden to the girls, she announced that she was going to return to Bethlehem. Orpah stayed behind with her own family, but Ruth insisted on accompanying Naomi back to the land of her birth. It could not have been fun for Ruth to travel with this bitter old woman. Naomi had even changed her name to Mara (which means "bitter"). But, when they arrived at the time of harvest, I imagine that robins appeared in the field because there the Lord met Naomi's need and restored her hope to her.

After what can only be described as one of the weirdest love stories ever recorded, we find that Ruth was married to her kinsman-redeemer, Boaz. Over the course of time, Ruth and Boaz had a baby boy. The book ends at a point where Ruth has placed the new baby in the arms of Naomi. The neighbor women are heard to say, "May he be to you a restorer of life and a nourisher of your old age; for your daughter-in-law, who loves you, who is better to you than seven sons, has borne him." I think Naomi's hope was restored. That little baby, Obed, grew up to become the father of Jesse. And Jesse was the father of King David. Through trusting in God, Naomi became the great-great-grandmother of the most loved king Israel ever had.

One can almost imagine that Jeremiah 29:11 could have been written directly to Naomi: "I know the thoughts that I think toward you, says the Lord, thoughts of peace and not of evil, to give you a future and a hope." I wonder if that is why God has instilled in the robin the desire to migrate north sooner than the other birds—to remind us mortals that we have a future and a hope.

## Setting the Standard

Robins are considered to be large birds. In fact, their 10-inch frame is often used as a model against which other birds are measured. Some of my bird books describe other species of birds as "smaller than" or "larger than" a robin. It is as if this bird sets the standard.

Robins have another distinctive besides their early migration, their size and their red breast. It is the particular times of day that they choose to sing. Unlike our little goldfinch friends, they only sing at certain times. They pierce the dawn each day with their happy song, but then they do not sing the reprisal until dusk. It is as if they know that happiness at the beginning of the day will lead to happiness at the end.

It was nearly always the robin's song, from a nest in a tree just outside my bedroom window, that woke me as a child. I remember looking down into the nest from my window each day and checking on the beautiful little eggs' development. When it came time to paint my bedroom, I requested "robin's egg blue." To our amazement, that really was the name of a beautiful light shade of turquoise blue on the color chart at the hardware store. One day I was devastated when a cat devoured one of the newly hatched robin babies for breakfast. Though they had sung that morning at dawn, I wasn't surprised that Papa and Mama Robin didn't find it in their hearts to sing that evening. But the next morning found them sharing their message of hope with the world once again, in spite of the tragedy that had befallen their little family.

I remember not being able to sing or even listen to any music for quite some time after my dad's home-going. Dad had always been a song leader in church, so every song seemed to have a close connection and memory associated with him. His all-time favorite was an old gospel song popularized by George Beverly Shea of the Billy Graham crusade team. Dad often began a service by asking the congregation to stand and sing the chorus of "How Great Thou Art." I remember one time when he just did not feel that the congregation had put their hearts into it or given it their all. He stopped the music and said, "You can do better than that. Now, just rear back, and let loose and beller it out!" My girlfriend, Jan, and I were laughing so hard that we could not sing a note. My mother was mortified, but the people surely did sing.

For years after Dad's death, I could not hear that beloved old song without tears. But somehow that has all changed recently. Now, instead of crying, I find myself singing at the top of my lungs on "How Great Thou Art." For I no longer think back to the days when Dad was alive on earth but focus on the fact that he is still alive in heaven. Truthfully, he is more alive there than he ever was here. So, like the robin does at eventide, I want to reaffirm the song that Dad taught me to love.

God truly is great and worthy to be praised. And because of the great mercy He bestows on us, I have the wonderful hope of seeing my father again. Just like the robins come back in the snow early every spring, at some appointed time in the future, I will join my father in the choir around the throne of God. But we will not just sing at two appointed times each day. We will praise His name throughout eternity!

Chapter Ten

# *Canadian Geese*

On my front porch at our pastorate in the country, sat a concrete statue of a goose. In the Midwest, you can see these little 27-inch-tall replicas of the gorgeous big birds on many porches. And, like little girls' dolls of old, they are arrayed in wonderfully detailed clothing. It has become a game to dress your goose to fit whatever occasion arises. For example, on the Fourth of July, every self-respecting concrete goose will be in a red, white, and blue outfit—some even sporting Uncle Sam beards and stovepipe hats. In the month of May the geese are often dressed in mortarboards and graduation robes. At Easter time the goose sometimes sports bunny ears. At

Christmas she becomes Santa Goose. You get the picture. Indeed, in our area, every visit to a flea market or craft show will find at least one booth (but usually several) featuring the latest in "Front Porch Goose Attire."

We had one gentleman in that church, Daryl, who found this idea of dressing a goose to be particularly silly. So for the seven years we were there, he teased this pastor's wife about my participation in this innocent fun. Somehow my goose acquired the name "Gladys," and the jokes that were told about Gladys are too numerous to mention at this point. Suffice it to say that the whole congregation joined in the fun. One time when we opened our Christmas gift from the congregation, included in the box was a new dress for Gladys. Another time, on a very hot July Saturday, I dressed Gladys in a two-piece swimsuit, complete with sunglasses and a visor to shade her little concrete eyes. Imagine my surprise when I came home from church on Sunday morning only to find Gladys had been wrapped in paper toweling from head to foot because our jokester thought she was guilty of "indecent exposure."

Our first winter in that parsonage was a bitterly cold one. Daryl, who was our head deacon at that time, called to see if we needed anything and if we were keeping warm. I joked with him that Dan and I were doing fine but I felt really bad for Gladys because she remained on the porch in a completely vulnerable place, unprotected from the wind, sleet, and snow. As soon as the storm abated enough to allow travel, Daryl arrived, toting a little shed he had constructed to shelter Gladys. Dan and Daryl began to discuss moving her from her current position on the edge of the porch to one where the little shelter would not interfere with the door. Then they went outside armed with shovels and began to brush the snow away from the concrete goose. Suddenly I heard uproarious laughter from the porch. I ran to check on the commotion and saw Daryl and Dan picking themselves up from the deep snow. The top half of Gladys the goose was beside them in the snow, while her feet were still firmly planted (encased in ice) on the porch. I now had a paraplegic goose. Amidst the laughter, Daryl said that he could take an old lawnmower apart and build a wheelchair for the goose. But another man in our congregation came through with a better plan. Jim performed major surgery (with the help of some ready-mix cement) and reattached the goose's legs to her well-dressed body. And so the saga of Gladys the goose continued all the time we lived on Cowpath Road.

Perhaps the practice of dressing geese has become such a phenomenon in our area of the Midwest because we are on direct flight patterns of the beautiful Canadian geese migration. Every man, woman and child in Ohio has probably seen the big "V"-shaped patterns of birds flying overhead each spring and fall. Nearly every hamlet or village that is big enough to have a park with water can boast several families of Canadian geese that choose to live nearby. Every child in our state has probably fed stale bread crumbs to geese and encountered the almost completely tame demeanor of the ones that live in the parks. From the top of their black heads to the bottom of their webbed feet, they are beautiful birds. Among the largest of waterfowl, their distinctive white cheeks and band under their chin seem to set off their black bills. It is my fervent hope that as we so often have the opportunity to view these regal birds, we will take a few minutes to ponder their lifestyles. For there is much we can learn about service from geese.

## Servants Extraordinaire

The first lessons are taught by the mother and father geese who are expecting imminent hatching of their goslings. From the time the eggs are laid, the mother goose constantly watches over them. She pulls downy feathers from her own breast to line the nest and cushion the eggs from any shock. In fact, she pulls so much down that she will eventually have a bare patch on her breast. Ornithologists refer to this bare area as her "incubation patch." As she sits on the eggs, she places this bare patch against each egg in turn so that her body heat can be more easily transferred to the eggs. The mother goose is also so smart that she periodically turns the eggs over so that every area is warmed in turn.

Recently, we had missionaries from Spain visiting with us. Their teenage daughter used a word I had never heard before as she referred to her friends in Spain. Ashley told us how she had to be constantly on her guard because her "pre-Christian" friends were watching every move she made and judging all Christians by her example. I thought it was a neat concept that those we are trying to witness to and lead to a knowledge of the Savior are "pre-Christians." (It's wonderful to learn from a teenager how to care for those "eggs" that we are praying will hatch soon!)

When the eggs hatch, both of the parent geese stay very close to the goslings, protecting and teaching. After the birds have a few days to "get their feet on the ground," Mama and Papa lead them to the water. As they go on their first swims, Daddy Goose swims in the lead. The babies are in a line in the middle. And Mommy is always seen bringing up the rear. When Mommy senses danger from beneath, perhaps a turtle or a big fish that could nip her darlings, she signals to her mate. Oh, the furor created as the papa goose swats wildly at the water and honks loudly! Any predator is likely to dive far below the surface of the suddenly churning water. And the goslings just swim along, never knowing that their lives were endangered. To those who have been privileged to watch this scene unfold, one fact is abundantly clear. The mother and father goose each "know their place" and do not fuss about it. They seem to sense that their babies need them to serve in the positions for which their Creator God has given them the instincts.

Some call me old-fashioned, but I am also convinced that men and women have God-given equal but different areas of service, both in their biological families and in the broader arenas of the spiritual family. When the man in a family refuses to be the protector and provider, it often leaves the children and the mother in disharmony and fear. When a mother, on the other hand, wants to be the one squawking and flapping her wings, there is a dissatisfied husband and frightened children riding in her wake. The church where I spent my formative years was very careful that men were in positions of leadership over boys and women taught and nurtured the girls. Every youth activity was directed by couples, so that both genders had someone to emulate and turn to with their problems. Like the geese that we watch as they swim, the children knew the rightful, biblical role of men and ladies. It seems to me that all churches would be better off if men and women were willing to serve in the roles God has ordained for them and clearly outlined in His Word.

## Flying in Formation

Perhaps the most startling lesson we can learn from

geese is one that can be easily observed by simply tilting our heads skyward as they fly over in their famous "V" formations. If you happen to be watching at exactly the right moment, you will be privileged to see a delicate change in the power position that takes place numerous times on their long migrations. The lead goose will simply begin to flap his wings more slowly and fall back to the end of one of the legs of the "V," allowing the next goose in line to take the point. Having seen this happen a few times, I began to wonder why. My research repeatedly uncovered the same amazing story of how the geese fly.

Scientists say that it is a matter of survival. The birds are traveling into the wind, which creates enormous friction against their wings. Somehow they have discovered that if they fly in formation, they form an ever-moving wall to block the wind which enables them to lessen each bird's tiring efforts. Now, obviously, the bird that is facing most of the wind's friction is the one at the "corner" of the wall, the center of the "V." So the lead bird is causing the wind to break more gently around the other birds in the formation, performing a valuable service to his whole flock. No bird could sustain the power needed to break that wind barrier for the entire length of their flight, so the birds wisely take turns in the lead.

The other strange part of a flock of geese flying overhead is heard rather than seen—all the birds except the lead bird are honking nonstop! On our quiet country road, a flock of geese can be heard approaching long before they can be seen. They create quite a cacophony of noise. Again, I wondered, "Why?" According to my research, it appears that the birds that are forming the arms of the "V" are encouraging the lead bird that is facing the wind by honking their support. I imagine they are saying things like: "Hang in there." "You can do it." "Only a few more miles and then it will be Charlie's turn." "Keep on keeping on!" "Attaboy!"

Now it would be easy for me to imagine that once the lead bird finally gives in and drops back to allow the next bird to become the wind-breaker, he would be exhausted. So, I wrongly assumed that when he dropped back, he would only use his energy to fly for awhile and not join in with the other birds who were honking their support. I was wrong. Scientists tell us that immediately after the lead bird becomes a follower, he begins to honk and encourage his fellow goose to continue the flight and lead the group to the proper spot for the next resting place.

We humans need to learn the lessons taught by the geese as they fly. Why is there often such a striving for leadership positions? Why is it so hard for someone to admit that they need a rest from leading and then to step down to allow others the opportunity to try their wings? And then, if we are willing to step down, why do we not immediately get behind the new leader and "honk" our support, rather than remaining quiet or, even worse, biting them in their backs?

In one of my husband's pastorates, we had a relatively new goose in our flock. He had been a growing Christian for a number of years and was ready to try his hand at a leadership role in the church. He had recently been appointed to serve in the role of deacon and was so excited and wanted to serve well. However, the man who had been serving as a deacon for many years was not willing to lend his support to the new guy in any way, shape or form.

Communion Sunday had arrived and the deacons were supposed to serve the elements to the congregation. Our new goose came to church that Sunday in a new suit and tie, spit shined from the top of his well-combed hair to the toes of his shoes. I had to smile to myself to see one so eager to look right as he served the bread and the cup. The organ was playing softly as the men made their way to the front of the church. As is the custom in our denomination, the Communion table had been spread with plates of broken bread stacked atop each other and trays of little cups of grape juice, also stacked together. A freshly ironed white cloth was draped over the top of the entire table.

The new deacon and the old deacon were paired to serve on the middle aisle, which gave them the responsibility of removing the white cloth from the table. The seasoned deacon picked up his end of the cloth at the crease in the middle, thinking to lift it by the crease and then grasp the outer edges with his other hand. Our new goose was so nervous he had not watched his former leader, so he picked up the cloth by the outside corners, thinking that he would bring the corners together to begin the ceremonial folding of the cloth. The older deacon's face turned a deep shade of purple as he cleared his throat fiercely. There was a brief awkward moment as the new deacon realized his mistake, adjusted his hands, and the cloth was folded neatly and the service continued. If I had not been in my assigned pastor's wife seat, I doubt even I would have noticed the brief struggle. Few people in the congregation saw the bobble, and those who did probably were thinking how nice it was to see our new deacon learning the ropes. The cloth was laid aside and the men passed the plates of bread and the trays of juice without further incident.

Imagine our horror when, immediately after the service, we saw the old leader of the church grab the new leader's lapel and take him outside. What ensued can only be described as a catastrophe of major proportions! God's heart must have been broken as the elder deacon proceeded to shout and gesture violently about how embarrassed he had been by the new man's stupidity. "Don't you have eyes? Haven't you ever watched how it is done? That was a mess!"

As is so often the case, it fell to my husband (the pastor) to do damage control. He apologized to our new deacon for the actions of the other man and confronted the older man about how wrong he had been. I wish I could say that the older gentleman realized the error of his ways and got at the end of the formation to honk his support for the newly appointed leader. However, what ended up happening was that the younger fellow eventually left the church—a broken man—convinced that he was not worthy of a leadership position. And, so, the "V" formation of that congregation never quite recovered.

Both of these men have since come to the end of their lives. I have often wondered if they are in heaven together, and if so, do they ever have the opportunity to serve together up there. I am pretty sure that it doesn't matter which way a cloth is folded when it is lifted from a Communion table. I am also quite sure that the lesson of service we could learn from the geese is that when it is time, we need to slip back into a less prominent place and honk our approval to the person who is just learning his job.

We also need to learn that the younger goslings are constantly watching the behavior of the older geese. On that horrible day in our church when the two men were outside the building, a little boy came into the foyer and shouted, "I think there's gonna be a fight in the parking lot!" It is hard to imagine what a younger goose would think if it watched two grown geese at the front of the "V" honking at each other, "I am not going to move back! I am the leader and I intend to continue to lead until I die. Just stay back there and honk your support." Instead, it would appear that what happens is the lead goose says to his neighbor, "Your turn, buddy. Just keep us on course, and I'll honk for all I am worth to help you."

There is one group of highly visible Christians that seems to have learned the lessons taught by the geese. If you have ever watched one of the countless Gaither Homecoming videos, you see this lack of struggle for the key positions beautifully portrayed. Some of the people on the videos are always just the supporting choir behind the more well-known singers, and yet they sing with their whole heart. The microphone is passed from person to person, and I have yet to see one of them stand up and say, "Hey, Bill— that's not fair! You are letting this young upstart sing my solo." Instead what I have often observed is the older singers wiping away tears as they nod in agreement with the words being sung. It would appear that they willingly allow the new geese to take the point position and lead us all to higher and higher plateaus of worship.

Jesus was confronted by a "mother goose" (no pun intended) one day. The mother of Zebedee's sons came to ask Him if He would grant that James and John be allowed to sit on special thrones at Jesus' right and left hands in the kingdom. Jesus' reply to her is a lesson in serving. He told her that the one who would be first should be last. If geese had been flying overhead that day, He could have pointed upward and said, "Watch how they do it. Learn from them."

I don't think it is any accident that within just a few days after Jesus had overheard another discussion among His disciples about who should be the greatest, He entered an upper room, took off His garment, picked up a basin and towel and knelt to wash each of their feet. By humbling Himself and taking on the job of a servant, He showed His disciples that we ought to be willing to serve in whatever capacity the heavenly Father asks of us. Whether it is lining the nest around the "pre-Christians" with the downy feathers of kindness, knowing our place in line as we swim in the world of predators, or acknowledging when we should take the lead of the flock and when we should drop back and honk our support to the leader, I hope we can learn the lessons of service just half as well as they are known by the regal Canadian geese.

## Chapter Eleven

# *Eagles*

*I* don't imagine there is an American alive who has not, at one time or another, been intrigued by the impressive bird which is our national symbol— the mighty bald eagle.

Perhaps more songs and poems have been written about this bird than any other. It is pictured on our money, stamps, flags, buildings, t-shirts, hats, banners, and even airplanes. Depending on the climate of the times, it has been used as either a symbol of war or of peace. Country singers croon about "the eagle flying," meaning America is on its way to seek retribution for the attacks of September 11, 2001. Children are taught in elementary school about the magnificent bird being an endangered species, a symbol of America that we should all seek to protect. Obviously, I have never had a bald eagle come to my window bird feeders, but any book about birds would be incomplete without a reference to this species.

Thankfully, I do know a place where one can view the bald eagle in an "up close and personal" environment. In Pigeon Forge, Tennessee, near the Great Smoky Mountain National Park, is an amusement park called "Dollywood." At the very back of this park, away from the hubbub of the rides and country music shows, the visitor steps into a totally different environment. It is shady and quiet and seems peaceful compared to its surroundings. A brief glance upward will reveal that the huge trees and wild-looking landscaping are all enclosed with a type of fencing. Somehow the fencing does not seem as obtrusive as you would think, for you soon learn that you have entered an eagle sanctuary. If you take the time to read the many huge signs that are placed along the quiet walkway, you learn that this wildlife sanctuary was begun to help save the American bald eagles.

On our first visit my son was upset and said, "They ought to be allowed to fly free. They should not be kept inside these cages, even if the cages are absolutely huge." I was inclined to agree with him and was disgusted by the idea that the amusement park was making money by caging some of these treasures of creation. But we came upon a person who worked there who immediately relieved our distress. She told us that the only birds in the sanctuary are ones that have something wrong with them. They bring them to Dollywood and give them excellent veterinary care. As soon as it is possible, if the birds can be rehabilitated, they are released back into the wild. Some of them would die if set free, due to damaged wings, beaks, or talons. These are the ones who will live the rest of their lives in Dollywood, where they are pampered as they are used to teach the public about the plight of the great birds. So we were appeased and relaxed to enjoy the learning atmosphere in this unique place.

The first thing we learned is that the bald eagle is not really bald. It got this nickname because its head is white, in stark contrast to its dark body. The tip of its tail is also white. We learned that a full-grown eagle can have a wing span of eight feet, making it one of the largest birds in the raptor family. I was amazed to learn that an eagle's eyes are bigger than mine and approximately six times more effective at long-distance vision. (Actually, since I am very nearsighted, the eagle can probably see about 30 times better than I can!) As we stood less than three feet away from a bald eagle, we could see the mighty talons of his feet. There were three forward-pointing toes and one pointing to the rear. At the end of each there is a claw that can measure up to two inches. Between those feet and the ferocious-looking yellow beak, it was easy to see why America had chosen the bald eagle to represent her strength.

The eagle sanctuary has a small stage area surrounded by seats made of logs sawn in half, reminding me of days long gone by at youth camp. When we arrived, a program was about to begin called "Birds of Prey." We sat down and learned all sorts of facts about everything from condors to buzzards. The climax of the program came when we were told to sit perfectly still. As music of America played, a wonderful bald eagle skimmed less than a foot above our heads and flew to the podium set for him on the stage. We learned that since this eagle had been injured in a way which would make living in the wild impossible for him, the staff there had worked with him until he was now almost tame. This same eagle has been used to fly into stadiums at the beginning of Super Bowl football games, baseball World Series, and other venues. He is quite a show bird, and the applause as he flew back to the trainer was deafening. I am thankful that the Dollywood Eagle Sanctuary exists to enlighten Americans about our national symbol.

## Learning to Let Go

With further research, I discovered that the eagle is mentioned at least 34 times in the Bible. So it would appear that God also thought there were things we could learn from this bird. As I have continued to study the eagle, one aspect of its life stands out above all the rest—it is a bird that knows when and how to cut the proverbial apron strings and let go of its young. Perhaps we humans could study how the eagle does it and then try to imitate what we see.

Eagle mamas usually lay two or three eggs in the magnificent nest, which is high in the branch of a tree or strategically placed in a rocky outcropping. The higher the nest from the ground, the easier it is for the young eagles when it is time to leave. Mama sits on the eggs, diligently keeping them warm and protecting them from predators which might decide to invade the lower regions of the nest. Eventually the tiny eaglets peck their way into the daylight and then a feeding frenzy ensues. Mama and Papa take turns going for fresh kill and feeding the quickly developing birds. During this time, when the babies are very young and vulnerable, the parent birds often spread their huge wings over the nest, protecting their young from the strong sun and the storms which hit them full force in the high nests.

Observers have also noticed that during the time when the eaglets are tiny, the mother and father bird curl their talons into a ball and walk about the nest on what has to be a very uncomfortable ball of needle sharp claws. Evidently they do not want to take a chance on their claws harming one of the babies.

By the time an eagle is six weeks old, it is nearly the same size as its parents. In the next few weeks, the downy feathers are all replaced by the slotted wings so characteristic of this bird. When it is 10 to 12 weeks old, it can successfully leave the nest and live on its own—for it will have been taught to hunt and how to kill and provide for itself.

From week eight and onward of the baby's life, the parent birds leave it more and more to its own devices. People who have been privileged to study this phenomenon relate that the baby eagle seems to perform a ritualistic exercise in preparation for its first flight away from the nest. Since the nest measures anywhere from six to nine feet across, the baby begins by hopping back and forth from one side of the nest to the other. This hopping looks like the bird is on a giant trampoline, for the wind begins to catch beneath its wings and carry it ever higher with each hop. Birds have been observed hopping as much as 15 feet up out of the nest.

When the parents see this begin to happen, they cut back drastically on the food they bring to the nest for the baby. Researchers have observed the parent birds flying by the nest, carrying a fresh kill. The babies will squawk like crazy, seeming to beg for the food. But the parents do not relent. They tempt the baby bird to take the plunge.

And it can be quite a plunge. That first hop out of the nest must look like the first hill on a huge roller coaster to the baby eaglet. But fear is soon dissipated when it realizes that Mama and Papa Eagle have been there all along and will not allow their baby to hurt itself. Some people incorrectly think that the larger birds will fly beneath and catch a falling baby eagle. This is not altogether correct. What the parent bird will do is fly very close alongside the fledgling bird. The action of the parent bird's wings flapping causes little whirlpools of air which will give the baby bird extra lift power, enabling it to fly high.

In Deuteronomy 32, Moses sang a song relating how God has cared for the children of Israel. In verses 11 and 12 he said, "As an eagle stirreth up her nest, fluttereth over her young, spreadeth abroad her wings, taketh them, beareth them on her wings: So the Lord alone did lead him..." Evidently Moses had been given the opportunity to observe an eagle as it cared for its young, spreading its wings in pro-tection. But notice that the verse says the eagle stirs up her nest. Evidently the mama eagle that Moses had watched had gone to the extremes that my research told me they will. If necessary, the parent eagle will nudge the baby out of the nest. While this seems cruel, one only needs to read the rest of the verse to realize that the adult eagle immediately flies alongside the baby so that the stir of air created by its wings will provide the needed updraft for the baby to begin to learn to soar.

I feel very privileged in that I know two people whose lives remind me in so many ways of the bald eagles. Alex and Theresia Fellows are the first missionaries I ever met. They have been serving the Lord in tribal regions of Ethiopia for more than 50 years.

Alex is a native of Australia who carries that wonderful "down under" accent to this day. When we first met them as a child, I thought he was perhaps the most handsome man I had ever seen. He is quick-witted and has cavernous dimples in his cheeks. I suppose I had an awful crush on him when I was about 12 years old. He seemed big and strong, but most of all, godly. Theresia is little and dark-complected. She is nearly the exact opposite of Alex. She is shy and quiet and serious-minded. I often wondered how they got together, for they seemed an awful mismatch, unless you spent some time with them and realized that they offset each other in ways that would only enhance their ministry.

When they were young, they took their six children with them to Africa. Like many missionaries, they served for four years overseas and then went home for one year to visit their supporters and report on the victories and trials they had experienced. One of their little eaglets died in Ethiopia. I remember wondering if they would be so distraught that they would return to the States. Obviously, I did not understand the depth of their commitment to bring the Gospel to the lost. As the other children grew up and reached high school age, one by one they would be left in America to study. These dear parents loved their children every bit as much as anyone else, but they loved and trusted the Lord more. They knew that their children had only been loaned to them. They knew that their job was to raise them to the point that they would be able to "fly on their own" and then urge them to leave the nest. I am sure that their hearts were heavy as they headed back to Ethiopia each time with one less child. But they knew that they had done all they could to raise the children in the "nurture and admonition of the Lord," and it was time to allow them to try their wings. At the end of each furlough, they would "fly beside" the fledgling that was to be left behind, making sure the child had the skills necessary to survive in America. And the children were not left alone—they were entrusted to valued friends and family who could care for them in their parents' absence.

Over the years I had lost contact with this family, but often wondered how they all were doing. Through a strange set of circumstances, we have now been reunited with these dear friends. Alex and Theresia are now in their early 80s. Their health is not what it once was, but they continue to serve the Lord. And yes, they continue to go to Ethiopia! I asked him when they are going to retire and his answer was vintage Alex. He said, "How can I retire and take my ease here in America as long as there is one Ethiopian who has not heard about Jesus?"

I asked about their children, thinking probably the children had hated being "pushed from the nest" and perhaps would have turned against the Lord as a result. I learned that the oldest son is a vascular surgeon who makes his home in Delaware. The next son works for an aluminum recycling ministry and lives in Canada. Their daughter lives in Georgia. One son lives in Australia where he continues to serve the Lord, after having served as a missionary for awhile. And the last son is a missionary in Ethiopia. They smiled shyly as they stated that "God has taken care of each of our children." They recently had a family reunion with many generations of choice servants from all over the world present.

Some people seem to think that if their children even move into the next county they would never survive. Since our children live in South Carolina and Maryland, I can attest to the fact that a parent can survive when their eaglets jump out of the nest. All we are required to do is to be "the

wind beneath their wings" for awhile—and then it is our job
to let go. Rather than cling to our children, we have chosen
to follow the example set by the eagles and by Alex and
Theresia Fellows. We agree with the Apostle John when he
states, "I have no greater joy than to hear that my children
walk in truth" (3 John 4).

Since they have unknowingly mimicked the eagles in
the rearing of their children, it does not seem strange that
God has granted Alex and Theresia such vigor and strength
in their old age. They seem to be the living embodiment of
the beloved verse found in Isaiah 40:31: "But they that wait
upon the Lord shall renew their strength; they shall mount
up with wings as eagles; they shall run, and not be weary;
and they shall walk, and not faint." God has definitely given
them the ability to mount up with wings. I can only hope to
be soaring as they are when I am in my 80s.

There's an old fable written by that world famous person
"Anonymous." The story goes like this:

A man found an eagle's egg and put it in a nest of a barnyard hen. The eagle hatched with the brood of chicks and
grew up with them. All his life, the eagle did what the barnyard chicks did, thinking he was a barnyard chick.

He scratched the earth for worms and insects. He
clucked and cackled. And he would thrash his wings and fly
a few feet in the air.

Years passed and the eagle grew very old. One day he
saw a magnificent bird above him in the cloudless sky. It
glided in graceful majesty among powerful wind currents,
with scarcely a beat of its strong golden wings. The old eagle
looked up in awe.

"Who's that?" he asked.

"That's the eagle, the king of the birds," said his

neighbor. "He belongs to the sky. We belong to the earth—we're chickens."

So the eagle lived and died a chicken, for that's what he thought he was.

How sad when we who are children of the King live as chickens when we could fly with the eagles.

Perhaps there is one thing sadder: when we are too "chicken" to bump our children out of the nest, so consequently they never fly at all.

Chapter Twelve

# *Doves*

One of the birds that is frequently seen all over North America, but rarely, if ever, at a backyard bird feeder, is the amazing mourning dove. Aptly named because of its mournful call of "oo-ah, coo, coo, coo," the mourning dove is a ground feeder. It is a bit heavier than most of the birds that come to my feeder. The length of its body seems out of proportion with the size and placement of its neck and head. I don't know if that is the reason it does not try to perch on the precarious feeder, or if it is just an instinct given by our Creator. What I do know is that the ground immediately beneath our feeder is often covered by a group of doves, feasting on the seed that has fallen to the ground—the leftovers of what the other birds eat.

Scientists tell us that doves are among man's best friends in the bird world. They eat seeds of weeds and pest plants. While they also love to eat corn, wheat, oats, barley and rye, they wait until the field has been harvested before invading it to search for food. Rather than damaging the crops by breaking off the stalks or scratching for their food, they pick the remaining seeds off the ground after the harvest is complete.

As agriculture has intensified over the last few hundred years, the population of mourning doves has increased proportionately. So, while some birds scramble to always keep away from man, the mourning dove seems to have decided that adapting to the changes that take place around it is the smarter course to take. Just as a dove will avoid the field when a combine is busy gleaning the harvest, the dove will also avoid the area under our feeder when there are other birds about. It seems satisfied with the food that is available to it, rather than always searching for bigger and better places to feed. As urban sprawl continues, and shrubs and plants—which would normally afford the dove not only food but quiet nesting places—decrease, the doves just find other things to eat and other places to build their nests. It is as if they will not be defeated or distressed. When I hear the haunting call of the mourning dove, I am reminded that Christians need to learn to adapt to many stress-inducing factors in our lives as well.

The seeds which are eaten by doves are hard for them to digest. So another way the dove adapts is by eating "grit" along with the seeds, which helps to grind them into digestible substances. The grit they eat depends on where they are at the time. The dove will use gravel, if it is along a country road or tiny specks of glass and cinders if they are in the city, to help with their digestion. Indeed, nearly any small, hard substance has been found in the crops of mourning doves, depending upon where they live. Rather than giving up when they cannot find the grit they prefer, they simply "go with the flow" and use whatever is available to them.

## Adapting

The Apostle Paul sets a fine example of adaptability. In Philippians 3:11, Paul writes to the believers at Philippi, "I have learned in whatever state I am, to be content." Early in our marriage, I used to wonder if the apostle might have written those words directly to me! By the time Dan and I had lived in California, Washington, Wisconsin, Illinois, and Ohio, I wondered if I would some day be able to say, "Having lived in every state in the Union, I can say that I have learned to be content in whatever state I am." Of course I knew in my heart that Paul was speaking of different states of being rather than actual physical "states," but when you are a young wife and mother feeling somewhat forced to move by your husband's career choices, it is hard to stay focused on how to adapt like the mourning doves do.

When people discover that in 36 years of marriage Dan and I have moved 20 times, they are amazed. One lady asked, "How have you maintained your sanity?" Others just shake their heads and exclaim that they had been born, grew up, and lived their entire lives within one mile of the home in which they currently lived. Then it is our turn to ask, "How have you maintained *your* sanity?" We laugh as we explained that some of the moves have been by personal choice, but many of them were dictated either by Uncle Sam or by the "call of God" upon our lives into full-time pastoral ministry. Women have told me they are thankful they have never been asked to move so often. But I have to admit that I have enjoyed getting to meet people all over the country, learning different customs, and in general just doing as the mourning doves do—adapting!

Mourning doves migrate from the northern states to the Southeast and back each year. They usually fly northward so that they arrive in the area where they will raise their next families in late March or early April. Immediately upon arrival, the male bird will select a nesting territory. If other males come into this territory, he will peck them until they leave. His next act is to coo and perform a special flight pattern to attract a mate. When their "marriage" has been "consummated," the pair begins to build a nest. Unlike some bird mamas, Mrs. Dove is not very particular as to the placement of this nest. Mourning dove nests have been found anywhere from ground level to about 50 feet in the air and are loosely constructed of twigs. Some are on the ground; others are in shrubs; some are in the crotch of tree branches. In town, the nests are even built on buildings. Sometimes the pair of doves will simply "sublet" a place that has already been constructed by a robin or another bird of similar size. Evidently it is more important to the mama dove that she have a nest, than that it be of any particular size or built in any particular place.

As soon as the nest has been built or claimed, the female dove lays an egg. She begins to incubate that egg, knowing that another egg will come in a couple days. Mama and Papa Dove share the incubation duties and within two weeks they are rewarded with a couple of "squabs," as the baby doves are called. Squabs are probably more dependent upon their parents than any other birds, since they are born completely naked, blind, and unable to care for themselves in any way. But the squabs grow and develop very quickly as they are fed a nutritious liquid called "pigeon's milk." The pigeon's milk is secreted in the upper digestive tracts by both the parent birds. They feed it to the young by regurgitating it into their little beaks. It is hard to imagine that within two weeks of their first appearance in the nest— naked, blind, and completely dependent—the squabs have grown feathers, learned to fly and find their own food, and are ready to leave the nest. This fast transition from birth to independence is another way the doves adapt, so that Mr. and Mrs. Dove have the ability to raise as many as five families before they migrate to the south again in the autumn.

And so it appears that the adaptability of the mourning dove is the main reason their population continues to grow in North America. As long as there are weed seeds in the edges of fields, leftover seeds thrown on the ground from bird feeders, and places for them to throw together a quick nest, we will continue to hear them cooing to each other about their happy, albeit somewhat shabbily constructed, homes.

When Dan and I set up our first home in a trailer that measured 10 by 50 feet, it was the most beautiful place on earth to me. We now laugh about our furniture when we look at old photographs of that place in California. The furnishings that came with the home were a "lovely" tan plastic. We had no end tables, so we set Dan's green footlocker up on end and put a towel over it. Our red plastic 14-inch (black and white) television proudly graced the top of the towel. Like the mourning doves, what was important to us was just having a place to live. It didn't matter that it was substandard in many ways. We were together, and we were happy.

Last spring I was asked to speak at a ladies meeting in a secluded area of Michigan. Fortunately my husband was able to go with me on this trip, where we enjoyed getting to know Dick and Pat Black. Dick was the pastor of the church where I was to speak, and the couple served as our gracious host and hostess for the evening before the meeting. Not only did we get to know Dick and Pat, we were introduced to their small brood of Diamond doves. Dick had constructed a wonderful aviary, which sits in the corner of their dining room. A visit with them was accompanied by the constant cooing of their pet doves.

Dick was a bit of an expert on doves, and it was from him that I learned that doves are unique to almost all other birds in the way they drink. Any avid bird-watcher can tell you that most birds scoop water into their lower beaks and tip their heads back to swallow it. Doves, however, can dip their beaks into water and suck it up like a pump. Watching this happen in the Blacks' aviary, and also in my yard, always makes me think of Gideon's army. In Judges 7, we find the story of how God weeded the undesirables out of Gideon's forces. Gideon was told to choose only the men who "lap the water with their tongues, as a dog laps....putting their hand (full of water) to their mouth" (verses 5, 6). Presumably, these men would make the best soldiers because they were watchful even as they drank water. They had learned to adapt the way they drank to the ever present dangers around them. And so, it would seem, adaptability is a good thing in God's eyes. I do not know why doves drink differently from almost all other birds, but I assume it has something to do with adaptation.

## Pigeons and Doves in the Plaza de San Marco

Doves and pigeons have adapted so well to their surroundings that they have become a nuisance in a very beautiful tourist spot. Several years ago when our son was stationed in Germany with the military, it was our great thrill to be able to visit him. We took a military bus tour while in Europe, driving through Switzerland and into Italy. Our ultimate destination (and a place that will always be one of my favorite cities on earth) was Venice.

We enjoyed a tour which told us all about the ancient buildings along the Grand Canal and were serenaded by a handsome man dressed in black and white as we rode in his gondola. We watched as local artisans blew the famous Venetian glassware and saw the "Bridge of Sighs" where prisoners saw their last glimpse of daylight before being taken below the waterline to their cells, which often turned into watery graves. We toured the beautiful Cathedral de San Marco and listened to the clock that has never missed chiming in 500 years.

One of our happiest memories involves the extremely tame pigeons and their cousins, the smaller doves, that inhabit the Plaza De San Marco. Our son has always been an animal lover, and he was intrigued by the hundreds of birds in the plaza. While others ducked their heads and ran, Kyer bought handfuls of special corn that is sold in the plaza to attract the birds. We have one picture of him with birds on his head and shoulders and three or four on each hand as they dove for the corn. Unbeknownst to the birds, the corn was laced with some chemical birth control. (Due to the overpopulation of the pigeons, man is forcing them to adapt by slowing their rate of birth.)

Since that happy time, our son has fulfilled a lifelong dream and now works with animals full-time as a Veterinary Technician. He is the only technician at the clinic where he works who makes friends with birds—the others prefer not to deal with canaries, parakeets, cockatoos or mynahs. A very sick parrot recently spent some time at the clinic. After the medicine had done its job, it was time for the bird to be released to its owners. Imagine Kyer's surprise when that bird paid him the ultimate compliment. It hacked and re-gurgitated its food, put the yucky stuff in its claw and proudly presented this "gift" to Kyer. In the world of pet birds, this phenomenon usually only happens when a bird has grown to love its owner over a period of years. Evidently, our son definitely has a way with birds! I wonder if it began with the pigeons and doves in the Plaza de San Marco in Venice.

## God's Special Place for Doves

A country gospel song extols the fact that God seems to have a special use for doves. Sonny James' classic hit "On the Wings of a Dove" tells about two places in Scripture that refer to a dove. One verse of the song is about Noah searching for land, and how God used a dove to show him that the waters had dried up enough for him and his family to leave the ark (Genesis 8:12 and 13). Another verse of Mr. James' song tells about how the Holy Spirit appeared as a dove at the time of Jesus' baptism (Matthew 3:16). Indeed, there are many symbolic references to the Holy Spirit as a dove in the New Testament. Perhaps that is why every episode of the popular television series "Touched by an

Angel" had a white dove flying away at the end, to signify supernatural intervention in people's ordinary lives. As Mr. James suggested in his song, we Christians need to remember that when troubles surround us, God will send down His love as if it were "on the wings of a snow-white dove."

## Wisdom in Adapting

Doves exhibit one other characteristic which always brings a smile to my lips. Perhaps more than any other bird, they have a funny way of walking. Their heads bob forward and backward with each step they take. One of my favorite teachers in high school was our band director. His walk was very dove-like. His head bobbed with each step he took. In fact, anyone who knew him could tell you that even if he was far away and you could not see his face, you could recognize him by his walk. Those of us in the band were allowed to call Mr. Utendorf by a nickname—"Mr. Glen." Each band member knew that we were important to Mr. Glen as individuals. We knew that if we had a problem, we could go to him with it. He not only taught us music. By the way he approached life, he taught us that adaptability was a goal to be aimed at. It was one he had achieved.

Glen Utendorf is the most musically gifted man I have ever known. Not only could he play almost every instrument in the band, he could also sing and write music. In fact, he wrote almost everyone of the many football shows that our band did over the four years that I was in high school. He arranged the music and the precision drills we marched as we played the music. One of his signature arrangements was a special version of the song "Bye Bye Blues." The band would play and march to the tune he had arranged as a regular John Phillips Sousa-style march, until we came to what he called a "break" in the music. At that point, the musical style changed. For a few bars it became a waltz. He had devised a special three-part step for the band, where we would point, shuffle, and then kick each foot to the rhythm of the waltz. It was really very striking to watch and I have never seen any other band do that step. Except once!

Our band went to band camp each summer to learn our football shows. One time as we were working on "Bye Bye Blues," the director of a rival band stopped by the camp and watched us rehearse. That fall we went to the biggest contest of the year. The contest was always won by either that rival band or us. They were to go first on the program. We were all seated and ordered by Mr. Glen to be polite and applaud them. In the middle of their program, they broke into *our* personal version of the song "Bye Bye Blues," complete with *our* waltz step. We were livid and began to shout, "They stole our program!"

Mr. Glen reacted much like I assume a dove would. Though he was visibly upset, his head bobbing faster than normal as he walked back and forth in front of us, he gained control of himself before he spoke. At the end of their program, he calmed us down and simply said, "Okay, we will just have to go out there and do our program better than they did it!" I don't think our band ever looked as sharp as we did that night. Our knees had never come up so high as we marched. Our turns had never been snappier. Our music had never sounded so good. Our "Mr. Glen's Specialty Waltz Step" was meticulously correct. And the applause and screaming were thunderous when the announcer said that we had won first place, while the rival school did not even place in the competition. Rather than *react*, our beloved band director had taught us to *adapt*. We adapted by doing our best, and we were rewarded.

Jesus told his followers in Matthew 10:16 that they should be as "wise as serpents and as harmless as doves." I pray that whenever I see or hear a beautiful mourning dove, I will remember that our Savior wanted us to adapt like the doves, so that He will be able to reward us some day.

Chapter Thirteen

# Crows

A trip northward out of San Francisco can bring the traveler into a beautiful little village called Bodega Bay. It is unfortunate that this pretty town is almost always associated with one thing and one thing only—Alfred Hitchcock's classic horror movie, "The Birds"! In the movie, thousands of crows descend upon this hamlet and proceed to destroy it. The residents of the town are at first mystified, then horrified, and eventually many die at the mercy of huge flocks of apparently demonic crows. The traveler to the town will find the old Potter schoolhouse still standing, and they will recognize the winding road leading into the town from the opening segments of the movie. While it may be a thrill to a movie fan to view the town where Mr. Hitchcock's first (and perhaps most widely remembered) full-length horror movie was filmed, it needs to be stated that crows have been given a "bum rap" ever since the movie hit the theaters. I have a lady friend who is extremely frightened of all birds—especially crows. In fact, she does not ever really relax and enjoy outdoor activities because she is constantly watching the sky for approaching birds. I assume it has something to do with her original viewing of the movie.

In our area, in the fall of the year, huge flocks of crows seem to descend from nowhere onto fields and wooded areas. Of all the domestic birds that I researched, crows are known to be the most flock-oriented. Rough estimates state that as many as 40,000 crows have been viewed traveling together.

I had watched Mr. Hitchcock's movie on one of the old movie channels available on cable TV one evening last year. The next morning I was driving along one of the country roads near our home. Imagine my surprise (dare I say, horror?) when the road in front of me was suddenly completely covered with the ominous-looking black birds. I tried to tell myself how ridiculous it was for me to slow down as I approached the birds. Certainly they would fly away and not attack my car as I had seen them do the night before on the small screen in our living room. And yet, my pulse was racing as I drove through the huge flock, their raucous caws drowning out the Christian music playing on the car radio. I could finally sympathize with my friend who fears birds.

## Einstein of the Bird Kingdom

Crows are large birds, measuring as much as 17 to 20

inches from end of beak to tail feathers. Of course, they are completely black from head to foot. Only their yellow eyes reflect any color. For this reason, it is nearly impossible to tell which crows are male and which are female. Another distinct characteristic of the crow is that it walks rather than hops. The crow not only has a much larger brain than other birds, but it appears that the bird uses it much more than its distant cousins, thereby earning it the nickname of "The Einstein of the Bird Kingdom."

The ability to manufacture and use tools correctly has long been thought to be a behavior pattern which was only associated with human beings and primates such as chimpanzees. However, there are now documented cases in which crows have also been observed "manufacturing" and using a tool to forage for food. Gavin Hunt, Ph.D., states in an article in the journal *Nature* that crows were seen plucking a twig with a particular shape and then stripping it of unnecessary leaves in order to use it to dig in the dirt and find insects, making them also the Henry Fords or the Thomas Edisons of the bird kingdom. They see a need for a way to do something, find a "tool" in nature to do it with, work on the "tool" to remake it to fit the need, and then use that same tool to meet the need. What an amazing feat for such a small, seemingly unimportant species to master!

Crows have even been observed arranging things in order of size. One crow was photographed trying to determine if there was a way for him to haul a number of berries to his nesting partner. The fast camera caught the bird moving the berries and trying differing combinations in his beak. Eventually the wise little bird realized that putting the smallest fruit in his mouth first and picking up the others in ascending order of size, was the most efficient way to complete his task.

Crows also seem to have the most developed system of all bird languages. Ornithologist experts can distinguish at least 50 different variations of the seemingly simple "caw" of these birds. By listening and observing how the flocks react to the differing calls, it has become known that slight modifications of the single syllable "caw" can mean such varying messages as "Danger!" "New food!" "I found water!" or even "All is well." When I learned these facts, it was easy for me to imagine that the huge flocks of crows I saw nesting in the area trees and on electric wires were holding classes in how to vocalize exactly what they meant to say. Or maybe they were having sessions of Crow Congress or meetings of the United Nations of Crows.

It is easy to imagine that sometimes the raucous cawing of the crows is simply laughter. Perhaps one of them noticed that Farmer Jim on Cowpath Road has put a scarecrow in his garden. One can imagine them jesting back and forth with statements such as, "Do they think we're foolish enough to believe that an object which never moves is any type of threat to our existence?" I wonder if they might not say, "Let's go sit on its arms just to prove that we are not afraid of it." Or maybe the wise little birds shout, "Why do you suppose they call it a scarecrow?"

## Cooperation

Crows are not usually frightened by people. What they are afraid of is large birds of prey—especially owls and hawks. In fact, one reason given for the movement of large groups of crows into cities is that owls do not usually live in towns. One of the ways we see crows cooperate with each other is in warding off their enemies. Indeed, whole flocks of crows will often harass, mob, and pester one owl until the owl will move to a different nesting area. Or, if it refuses to move, sometimes a flock of crows will peck an owl to death. Singly, they would be easy prey for the owl. But working together, they can win against their large enemy. The wise crows realize that there is safety in numbers.

The apostle Paul compared the Christian life to that of a soldier. Only through the strength found in numbers can an army be successful in its onslaught against the common enemy. The Bible clearly states that we Christians "are not to forsake the assembling of ourselves together as is the manner of some," but we are to meet together in order that we might exhort each other "and so much the more as you see the Day (of judgment) approaching" (Hebrews 10:25). It would appear that there are dangers in the world that we Christians need to unite to fight against, like the crows do against the enemy owls. We could certainly learn lessons about cooperation from the black birds.

Another observable phenomenon which happens repeatedly in a crow's life is that of helping the hurting. When one bird is injured in flight, usually at the hands of a human with a slingshot or a BB gun, many other birds will have surrounded it before it ever falls to the ground. They try to encourage it to keep on flying. Indeed, whole flocks of crows have been seen stopping to try to help an injured comrade.

If only we Christians could learn this lesson from the crows! It has often been said that the Christian army is the only one which routinely shoots its own wounded. We know several young women who have been through abusive situations in their marriages. One young lady sobbed in my arms and told me that after she finally got up the nerve to leave the man who was verbally and physically tearing her to shreds, she was told by another believer, "It is not ever scriptural for a person to walk out of their marriage." This young woman was devastated. She said that it was bad enough to know that her husband was likely to slap her around; but then when she went to church to try to seek solace from other Christians, she felt, by their words and actions, that they were slapping her just as hard. You would never see this happen with crows. When one is hurting, the entire flock rallies to their defense.

## Dealing With the Guilty

However, crows do not uphold a bird who is offending the understood law of the flock. There are orders given within the flock—jobs to do, as it were. One of the most important jobs is that of sentry. Whether you observe an entire flock of crows eating remaining grain in a recently harvested field or a small family of the black birds feasting at the dumpster behind the local McDonalds, you can usually see which bird has been designated to be the sentry. It will be perched a bit away from the rest of the crowd. Upon the approach of any imminent danger, the sentry crow will "go crazy" with the loudest cawing you have ever heard. I have observed this at a large puddle in our yard. When the birds are busily bathing or drinking there, one will be assigned to watch the area for enemies. If I let my dog out, the sentry crow will caw loudly and all the birds will immediately scatter.

People who study birds for a living wondered what would happen if the sentry was somehow distracted from his job, thereby allowing a fellow in his flock to be injured or killed. They spent hours watching and releasing potential enemies, then recording the results. It was discovered that crows will hold a type of "court session" for a bird that did not do its job. Many birds seem to "testify," and if the sentry bird is found guilty, no mercy is shown. The other birds will literally murder the offender, pecking it to death.

While I am not suggesting that Christians should hold court sessions and put an offending brother to death, I do believe the church of Jesus would be much healthier if the clear directives of Christ (found in Matthew 18:15-17) were put into practice. Some Christians today are so afraid of judging that we sometimes ignore or wink at situations involving Christians who are guilty of overt sin. Yet, the Bible teaches in 1 Corinthians 5 that it is our responsibility to stop having fellowship with a believer who is living in perpetual sin—not so the person will turn away from God, but so they will *want* to be restored. Even though crows have highly developed brains, of course they cannot possibly understand how to "restore" one who has been found guilty of sleeping while on sentry duty. The only thing they know to do is to kill the guilty bird. It's my prayer that those of us who name the name of Christ would obey what He tells us to do in Scripture and see restoration of a sinning brother take place.

My husband has had to take a strong stand against the all-pervasive sin of immorality in our world. Young people often come to him and ask him to marry them. After just a few questions, it becomes obvious that the couple is living together. Since this is a clear violation of Scripture, Dan refuses to marry cohabiting couples. This has caused heartbreaking results when the sinning believers refuse to turn from their wicked ways. But, the opposite is also true. We had two couples in one church who were very actively involved in ministry, but both of them were living in sin. Dan followed the biblical injunctive to confront them on this issue. Eventually, each person confessed the sin in their lives and changed. Later, after they had lived separately, they came back together in God-honoring marriages that have become shining examples to the community. I am thankful that my husband continues to pursue righteousness with crow-like determination. But perhaps more importantly, he knows how to extend grace to those who confess and return to living holy lives.

## Dealing With Death

Crows display their ability to cooperate with each other in the flock in one more amazing way. In fact, though it has been observed and reported in many respected journals and by some of the most well-known ornithologists, this practice of crows seems so human-like that it is hard to believe. Crows hold "funerals" for members of their flock who die. When a crow dies, the entire flock of birds seems to know it immediately. They all gather in surrounding trees, on wires, in the field—or if the bird's demise takes place in town, they will gather on buildings, cars, or whatever is in the area. The squawking caws are deafening. The screaming seems to go on and on. Then suddenly it all stops. There will be complete silence. The birds sit perfectly still and do not make a sound. After a minute or two, the raucous cawing begins again, and the flock disbands and flies off in many directions.

While I have never observed a "crow funeral," it has been clearly documented in so many places that I really believe it does happen. And the question begs to be asked: Why? Why would all the birds stop their constant search for food and gather together when one dies? Why would they all perch and scream for what seems to be an interminable amount of time? And then, why would they observe a few moments of complete and utter silence before winging their way to the sky again?

Of course there are no easy answers to these questions, since we cannot have a conversation with a crow. But I think it is a ritual that they have developed to honor the bird that has passed away. Much like the playing of taps or the bowing of heads in silent prayer at a human graveside, I believe the birds simply want to acknowledge that one of their own has died.

The television program "Star Trek" proclaimed each week that "space is the final frontier." I disagree. I believe that death is the final frontier. And I sometimes wonder why we fear it so much. Intellectually, I know that fear is a reaction to the unknown. But for those of us who are Christians, all we need do is read the Bible and suddenly death is not such an unknown. When someone we know dies, I believe that we should do like the crows do, and have a "service" to honor that person's life. Of course there will be mourning (like the raucous cawing of the crows). But it seems that we humans often get "stuck" in the process of mourning and never reach the stage where we can get back in flight and on with the business of living.

Have you ever wondered why John 11:35 records for us (in the shortest verse of the Bible) that "Jesus wept" at the graveside of his friend, Lazarus? He was God incarnate. He knew that He was going to bring Lazarus back from the dead. He knew that He was going to use Lazarus as an object lesson to teach His disciples and the others in Bethany that day about His power over death. Why then would He weep? I have always been taught that it was because He was empathizing with Martha and Mary. Or some have suggested that He was saddened by their lack of faith. I am currently reading a book about the life of Ruth Bell Graham, the wife of the famous evangelist, Billy Graham. She suggests a completely different reason for Jesus' tears at the grave of Lazarus. In one of her beautiful poems, she asks, "Could it be because He had to bring him back?" As God incarnate, Jesus knew what Lazarus was experiencing in heaven. He knew that Lazarus had entered the land where there is no more night, no more tears, no more pain, no more heartache, no more sickness—and, most importantly, no more sin! Perhaps the real reason the Son of God wept was because He knew Lazarus would not want to come back from that wonderful place.

And so, I hope that when my time on earth is done, my friends and family will follow the example set by the crows. You can have a brief service. You can shed a few tears. You can observe a few minutes of silence. But then, please fly away! Get back on with the business of living. For, where I am at that moment will be so much better than where you are. Do not get stuck in mourning. Move on, and live the rest of your life so that some day you can join me and all the millions around the throne of God where we will worship Him forever.

Chapter Fourteen

# The Great Speckled Bird

*I* sat in our living room at 6:15 P.M on a cool summer's evening. As we so often did, rather than run the air-conditioning, we had opened many windows throughout the house. I sat beside an open window reading, but I suddenly became aware of a quiet pecking noise. Looking out at the feeder, I saw a beautiful American goldfinch at the feeder. He was having a feast. No singing just now, for he was busy eating. In fact, I noticed that there was no other sound of any kind. It was always very quiet in the country, but I could usually hear crickets or birdsongs or locusts. If not that, then there was the hum of a tractor. Occasionally we could even hear the cows, which were a half a mile away. That particular evening, though, there was absolutely no sound except for the noise of the yellow bird pulling feed through the miniscule holes.

I was tired, so I leaned my head back and closed my eyes—thinking about the different types of birds in this book and all I have learned from them. I thought of how various people in my life, specifically in the many churches where we have been privileged to serve, have reminded me of different types of birds. Some displayed bad traits—more displayed good. But all of the different "birds" are God's children. All are part of the great "invisible church" which will someday be taken up to join our Lord in the air.

I let my mind drift and it seemed to go on a strange course. I thought of my first trip, at least 25 years ago, to Nashville, Tennessee. We had traveled with my parents who wanted us to see "The Grand Ole Opry." Mom and Dad had been there several times and had told us that this was not only a performance that we could watch, it was a live radio program. We loved country music and were hopeful that we would get to see some of the big stars perform their hit songs. The Opry house was nothing like I expected. There was a lot of hubbub on the stage between each "act"— changing of microphones and setups. Indeed, during some of the songs, there was confusion and unnecessary movements of extra people on the stage. I knew that the people in "radio-land" could not see this and did not know it was happening, but we had paid good money to watch this show and I did not like the casual, haphazard atmosphere of the performance. I felt that way until they introduced Mr. Roy Acuff, the "King of Country Music."

Mr. Acuff sang pure, old-time bluegrass music, with only

the accompaniment of some guitars and his own fiddle. From the moment he came on stage, I was mesmerized. All the unnecessary movements ceased, and everyone seemed to stand a little straighter and give him their deepest respect. He seemed very old, even then, with his white hair and rather shaky voice. But how that man could play a "fiddle"—and don't you dare call it a violin! What's more, when he wasn't playing it (and when the radio announcers were doing the commercials), he was balancing the fiddle first on his finger, then on his chin. Sometimes he did all sorts of fancy work with a yo-yo. He was an extraordinary showman. He was so loved and respected by all the other members of the Opry that the atmosphere during the segment he hosted was electric. He introduced singer after singer, calling them "boys and girls" and telling them to "sing the song that brought you here!" So, during his half-hour-long part of the show, we heard only huge hits, not insignificant new songs the singers were trying to launch. At the end of his segment, he spoke of his love for the Lord and said he was going to close this portion of the program with "my signature song." He looked toward the ceiling and held his fiddle at his side. In that rather scratchy voice for which he was famous, he began to sing the words Rev. Guy Smith had penned so many years before: "What a beautiful thought I am thinking, concerning the great speckled bird..."

It was only then that my thoughts seemed to make any sense to me. I now found myself humming "The Great Speckled Bird," and wondering what the song was really about. A little bit of research revealed that the song is based on a verse found in the Bible, in Jeremiah 12:9. The song compares the entire worldwide church of God to a great speckled bird. The lyrics are about how other birds despise her because she is chosen. I thought of how people of other religions sometimes hate Christians because we are so certain of our future with the Lord. If only they could understand that we are not proud or exclusive—the same Gospel which has been applied in our lives is available to them, if they can simply accept it by faith. Another verse of the song talks about how her wings shelter men of all colors and nations. And I smiled as I thought how her wings also shelter imperfect people—maybe that is the reason it is called a speckled bird. For, as everyone knows, we Christian birds are not perfect—we are just forgiven!

The chorus of Mr. Acuff's signature song is about how this great speckled bird is spreading her wings for a journey. Of course it is talking about the day described in 1 Corinthians 15:52, when we will hear the sound of a trumpet and all Christians will rise to meet Jesus in the air. Though I often like to compare myself and others to different kinds of birds (whether it be parakeets, bluebirds, turkeys, crows, or all the other species in between), what I am most thankful for is that I am a part of that "great speckled bird"—the Church of Jesus Christ!

# About the Author

Raelene Phillips began to write professionally in 1982, contributing short stories for children's Sunday School papers and writing for the radio ministry of the Children's Bible Hour in Grand Rapids, Michigan. She also wrote a trilogy of historical Christian romance novels, *Freedom in White Mittens, Freedom's Destiny Fulfilled,* and *Freedom's Tremendous Cost* (Bethel Publishing). Her other published works include *Where Is Your Pineapple? A Handbook on Hospitality* (Evident Press) and another book in the **All God's Creatures** series—*Puppy in the Pulpit* (Evergreen Press).

Having completed the requirements to become a C.L.A.S.S. Communicator, she is in high demand as a humorous Christian motivational speaker. Raelene is listed in *Who's Who of American Women* for 2004 and 2005.

Raelene and her husband Dan have been married for 36 years and have two grown children (daughter Sonya and son Kyer). Dan has been in full-time Christian ministry for 24 years, and Raelene has been actively involved in the church's ladies ministry, teaching, and music.

To contact the author for speaking engagements, please write: Raelene Phillips, 1109 West Robb Avenue, Lima OH 45801.